THE ESSENTIAL
BOGOSIAN

THE ESSENTIAL
BOGOSIAN

Talk Radio, Drinking in America, Funhouse & Men Inside

ERIC BOGOSIAN

THEATRE COMMUNICATIONS GROUP

1994

Bogosian, Eric.
    The essential bogosian : talk radio, drinking in America, funhouse, and men inside / Eric Bogosian.—1st TCG ed.
    ISBN 1-55936-082-8
    1. Monologues.   I. Title.
PS3552.046A6   1994
812'.54--dc20   93-51493
                                                                 CIP

Book design and composition by The Typeworks

First TCG Edition, May 1994

TABLE OF CONTENTS

FOREWORD

When I think about what kind of theater I would like to *make*, I think about what kind of theater I would like to *see*. And if you don't want to see what I like, don't bother coming to the show.

I want theater to wake me up, not lull me to sleep. My theater is not about fantasy, it's not about seduction. My theater is not an outline for a film. It is not a TV sitcom onstage. I want my theater to be an event. I want it to push limits, bite the hand that feeds, bang heads. It's about my fears, my ideas, my blind spots, my isolation.

Between 1976, when I moved to New York, and 1980 when I started writing the pieces in this book, I created (and either performed in or directed) over a dozen "performances." These include: *Sheer Heaven*, a play for Hispanic actors performed in Spanish for "anglo" audiences; *The New World*, a series of cliched and violent *tableaux* with a cast of sixteen; *That Girl*, a solo about sex; *Heaven, Heaven, Heaven*, an ensemble piece with slide projection, children and loud electric guitar; *The Garden*, performed on a ramp of mesh steel; and *The Ricky Paul Show*, the life and times of a misanthropic punk comedian and his back-up band.

I churned it out—however, whenever, and wherever I could. I especially liked performing "Ricky." His negativity was exhilarating. Then I switched gears and put together a "gallery" of men. This became *Men Inside*, the first in a series of solos: *Men Inside*, *FunHouse*, *Drinking In America*, and *Sex, Drugs, Rock & Roll*. (As I write this, I am finishing a new one: *Pounding Nails in the Floor with My Forehead*.)

I made these solos as little arenas of freedom. I could say what I wanted, do what I wanted, bounce around, break a sweat. When I first made them, they weren't very "polished" and I still fight the urge to smooth them out. I wanted the shows to be bigger than the words. I wanted the shows to be untranslatable into anything but performance.

The solo shows ran Off Broadway and created credibility for my work. This "credibility" led Joseph Papp to underwrite the ambitious production of *Talk Radio* at the Public Theater in the late spring of 1987. The play was optioned by a film producer and soon adapted for the screen.

At the end of 1988, I was introduced to the world as "Barry Champlain" via the film *Talk Radio*, and a new chapter in my life began. I had worked on film projects before and had even written a screenplay for a major studio, but *Talk Radio* changed my life. I got a new perspective on a world I could only imagine before. I had become part of something I had ridiculed.

Theater had been "home" for me since I was fourteen. It was the place where I felt most alive. My highest highs were in theaters, either onstage or in the audience. But theater seemed slow, square and out-of-touch with the world. Film seemed more exciting, more intense, "epic." Theater was pure, but elitist and precious. Film beckoned, like the siren song calling to the ships at sea. It promised beauty, but delivered the sharp rocks of the mass media.

Talk Radio and other experiences in the "screen trade" have sharpened this conflict and, at the same time, given me some insight. Theater/live performance remains the paramount aesthetic experience. At the same time film and TV are ridiculously exciting. Theater was love, film was rock 'n' roll. I want both. That's where I'm at today, still suspicious of the toxic mass media, and still unhappy with the turgid theater that dominates.

As an artist I am poisoned by mass media's attempt to translate my every effort into some kind of competitive action. In my life I'm going to make many things (hopefully), each one more or less fitting to the time and place in which I make it. There is no "winner."

The machinery of the mass media is emotionless and amoral. It can count admissions, rate box office, score demographics—that's it. It is powerful and it is cold. I live under the terrifying skies of mass media hoping to seize the lightning and use it for my needs. Ego being what it is, I hope to pass through the system unscathed. But who is the user, and who is the used? The more I am seduced by this way of looking at things, the more I become an adjunct to the machine.

All this leads to frustration, which leads to explosions of expression. Strangely, explosions can then be commercially successful and lead right back into the scary universe. I've taken such a path with my solos and the play *Talk Radio*.

The work in this volume is "essential" in my personal history because with these four shows I began a journey. I left being an anonymous artist downtown to become someone much more savvy to the rules of the media game. *Men Inside* introduced me to the national press, *FunHouse* was my first commercial run (at Actor's Playhouse in Greenwich Village), *Drinking in America* was a "hit" and *Talk Radio* a play adapted to film and distributed by a major studio.

Something in me wants to be "loved by millions," whatever that means. But as the bardos in the *Tibetan Book of the Dead* advise, I must ignore the mirage and walk through it. I imagine an audience filled with friends and then I try to please them.

ACKNOWLEDGEMENTS

This book is dedicated to my wife, Jo Bonney. She directed me in *FunHouse*, *Sex, Drugs, Rock & Roll* and the new show, *Pounding Nails in the Floor with My Forehead*. We work as a team and I can't imagine making the work without her. There is no "essential" Eric Bogosian without Jo Bonney.

Three of the pieces in this book were originally produced by the late Joseph Papp at the New York Shakespeare Festival. His moral example and his expectations of me set marks I will never reach. He and Gail Merrifield supported me and encouraged me in my most desperate hours. Jo and I will cherish his memory always.

My friend, Fred Zollo, produced *FunHouse* Off Broadway and directed the original production of *Talk Radio*. The play *Talk Radio* is dedicated to him. He and Nick Paleologus have been great producers and great friends.

Performance Space 122 has been my home downtown for a dozen years. All the work in this volume appeared there in one way or another. Special thanks to Mark Russell and all the good people there.

Thanks to Tad Savinar, who had the original idea that I do a piece about talk radio.

Also thanks to Wynn Handman, my director on *Drinking in America*, who gave me a home at the American Place Theater. He introduced me to the world with the help of Phil Rinaldi, my press agent, who has since become my friend and cherished advisor.

I would like to thank Oliver Stone and Ed Pressman for making *Talk Radio*.

I would like to thank the editor of the original editions, David Rosenthal, who endured me. Thanks to Michael Carlisle, who secured me. Thanks to Jon Trumper who has kept the faith. Thanks to Ron Taft who protected me. To Frank and Woji Gero who set me up. To my parents, Henry and Edwina, who made me. And thanks to Pat Sosnow, my stage manager, for coffee and cigarettes.

Finally, this business is a confusing thicket, one that requires a sharp eye, a clear mind and a strong machete. Thanks to George Lane, my agent, for being my guide.

TALK
RADIO

AUTHOR'S NOTE

Reading *Talk Radio* today is confusing. First of all, there are two *Talk Radios*: the play and the film. In this book is the play I wrote in 1987 with the help of Tad Savinar; my director, Fred Zollo; and the original Oregon and New York casts. If you pick up the video of the film I made with Oliver Stone, you will find a different script with basically the same story and characters. That screenplay is the work of Stone and myself, and the result is an edgier, darker exercise.

Talk Radio was not based originally on any radio personality. What I wanted to do was write something that dealt with John Belushi's death. I felt his terminal overdose was a result of his experience with the mass media. I share some traits with Belushi: ethnic and middle class with a penchant for dark humor and high-octane performance.

I didn't think I could do a piece about a comic, because I could never write material funny enough. But a talk-jock is a performer too, and although at the time I had no inkling of the wilder DJs on the air (like Berg, Stern, Dee, et al), when Tad suggested to me that I do a piece about "talk radio," it seemed like the perfect launching pad for an over-the-top, acerbic egomaniac.

Despite its title, *Talk Radio* is not an in-depth, researched, generic documentary. (There is no radio station set up like the one in the play.) Instead, I wanted to use the format, one few people had any sense of in 1987, as a launching pad to talk about my own ego and the mass media in general. I loved the notion of this vast landscape of people, the callers. And I wrote in archetype: Barry and every caller were meant to be instantly recognizable and familiar.

Coincidentally, when the play opened, a book showed up in the bookstores called *Talked to Death*, by Stephen Singular, about the life and assassination of Denver talk-jock Alan Berg. When I read the book I was impressed by the similarity between the real-life Berg and my fictional Champlain. When it came time to make the movie, we secured the rights to the book and Berg's life, and created a pastiche from the real-life tragedy and my play.

In the play, no one dies. In fact, because it is a play, the moment to moment texture of the thing is more in the foreground than the "plot." Basically, watching the play was something like being there in the studio with Barry, so to the degree Barry was entertaining, so was the play. (Larry Pine took over the role when I left, so I got to experience a wonderful "Barry" from outside looking in.)

The play is meant to stand as an abstract of a culture, not some kind of docudrama. Real talk radio in 1987 was a late-night phenomenon. What better place to examine a nation's soul? Every caller could present a different point of view, and so the play would become a kind of kaleidoscope. As it twisted and turned, the audience could meditate on how we think of ourselves as people, as a nation.

I had listened to numerous talk-jocks (particularly Bob Grant and Gary Dee) and drew from my pre-teen experience of the legendary Alan Burke and Joe Pyne (two TV talk guys from the sixties with razor blades for tongues). But when the movie came out, the strangest thing happened—a new guy had shown up and was making big waves soon after the movie came out; his name, of course: Howard Stern.

Howard Stern today is a big star because he's so brilliant at what he does. But at the time of writing this play, the notion that someone as acid-tongued as Stern would "go national," or have a public war with the F.C.C., or become more famous than most movie stars, was on the very rim of anyone's imagination, including, I'm sure, his own. To add the coincidences that he and Barry share this ethnic/hipster thing, are cynics and have a penchant for rock 'n' roll (Barry Champlain was using "Bad to the Bone" as theme music before anyone else) lay beyond all odds.

Is Howard Stern Barry Champlain? I hope not, for Stern's sake. As far as I know, this play is not based on one man's life; rather, I meant it to be a quilt of madness from the late eighties, a play about voices in the dark. Remember: sticks and stones can break your bones, but words cause permanent damage.

The original version of *Talk Radio* was produced in 1985 at the Portland Center for the Visual Arts through a grant from the National Endowment for the Arts and the Metropolitan Arts Commission.

The original New York City production of *Talk Radio* was first performed at the New York Shakespeare Festival, Joseph Papp, Producer, May 12, 1987. It was directed by Frederick Zollo. It was performed by (in alphabetical order): Linda Atkinson, Eric Bogosian, William DeAcutis, Susan Gabriel, Zach Grenier, Michele M. Mariana, John C. McGinley, Mark Metcalf, Peter Onorati, Robyn Peterson and Michael Wincott.

CHARACTERS
(In order of appearance)

SID GREENBERG	Financial Talk Show host
BERNIE	Sid's operator
SPIKE	Engineer
DAN WOODRUFF	Executive producer, WTLK
STU NOONAN	Barry's operator
LINDA MACARTHUR	Assistant producer of "Nighttalk"
BARRY CHAMPLAIN	"Nighttalk" host
KENT	Guest
DR. SUSAN FLEMING	Talk Show host
OPERATOR FOR DR. FLEMING	
CALLERS	

The set is a stripped-down version of a radio studio—WTLK, a "talk radio" station operating out of Cleveland, Ohio. Two console tables occupy the main space. One, stage left, faces the audience and is equipped with a small computer screen, a phone unit with buttons for several lines, and a studio mike on a "Luxo" armature. Two office chairs are on either side of the table facing the audience. This is the talk radio host's console. The second table, stage right, faces away from the audience and is equipped with a computer screen and keyboard, a larger phone unit, and a headset. This is the operator's console. Behind and above the operator's desk is a little balcony with three steps leading up to it. The balcony leads to a door, which in turn leads to the sound engineer's booth. The booth is separated from the main space by a large plate glass window. Thus the engineer can look out over the space and see both the operator and the host. In extreme downstage right is a coffee machine on a small table along with cups, sugar, and spoon and another office chair, where the assistant producer sits. Behind this chair is a coatrack. As the audience enters the theater the set is bathed in dim light. Soft "easy listening" music is played over the sound system. The set is empty. The music grows louder as house lights and stage lights fade to black. The music begins changing rapidly as if someone were switching channels, then finally "finding" WTLK. In black, an announcer's voice booms out.

ANNOUNCER'S VOICE Coming up in just a few minutes, "Nighttalk" with Barry Champlain right after the news and weather...and now, back to Sidney Greenberg and "Your Taxes and You."

Sid is heard in the dark, a nasal, clipped voice.

SID . . . All righty, now, Richard, are you still with me?

Stage light snaps on to reveal Sid Greenberg at the host's desk. He is hunched over the microphone, smoking a cigar. The desk is a mess of take-out containers and coffee cups. At the operator's desk sits Sid's assistant, Bernie, and in the engineer's booth sits Spike, the engineer.

  Sid speaks with a flowing energy that gives little room for the caller.

SID OK, now with the cash that you have in hand from the second mortgage on the first property, the property on the lake . . . you've either taken a second mortgage or completely refinanced that property. Now you have cash in hand. What are you gonna do with that cash?

RICHARD (*Caller*) That's why I—

SID Figuring the property is probably worth in the neighborhood of two hundred thousand, you pay off the existing mortgage of ten thousand bucks with a hundred-and-seventy-five-thousand-dollar refinancing loan. Simple arithmetic leaves you with a hundred and sixty-five thousand dollars. . . . Now you could *pocket* this money, but that isn't going get you *anywhere*. 'Cause you're not using the money! And the last thing you want to do is *sell*, 'cause that means *capital gains tax* and that means you gotta send a check to . . . yeah, you guessed it, our Fat Uncle in Washington. . . . Don't wanna do that, so hold on to that property! Now, . . . Richard, you still with me?

RICHARD Uh-huh.

SID Richard, do you have a paper and pencil? . . . Good, 'cause now we're gonna make some money! What you need is a tax break and some income, so you take that hundred and sixty-five thousand and you fly to Florida and you look for an office building going for somewhere in the neighborhood of one or two million bucks. You use that hundred and sixty-five thousand and the fifty grand your uncle left you and the hundred thou you're gonna make off the second mortgage on your house and you put that all together and you use that three hundred and fifteen thousand dollars as a *down payment* on the office building in, let's say, Cocoa Beach.

RICHARD Florida?

SID You take the income you make on the rentals in that building and put the excess income beyond your monthly finance payments on the two notes into either a zero-coupon bond or a T-bill—

RICHARD What about a Ginnie Mae?

SID Ginnie Maes, Fannie Maes, Willie Mays, you'll never lose with bonds. . . . Establish an annuity trust and your kids will have plenty when college days roll around *and* you'll be sitting pretty with a tax break in Florida, two places to go on vacation, and, *get this, Richard,* over two million dollars' worth of property. . . . Unbelievable, but guess what, Richard, using my method, you've just become a millionaire! How about that!

While Sid gives the last speech, Stu Noonan, Barry Champlain's operator, has entered and perched himself on the railing of the balcony, waiting for Bernie to vacate his seat.

RICHARD But what about—?

SID (*Cutting him off*) All righty, the big clock on the wall tells me that it's time to wrap up this episode of "Your Taxes and You" for this evening. Stay tuned for the news and weather, followed by some stimulating conversation from the master, Mister Barry Champlain. . . . I'm Sidney Greenberg, reminding you that "it's not how much you take, it's how much you take home." (*Stands, sticks his cigar in his mouth*) All right, we're off. . . . So . . . are we going from here?

Bernie has grabbed coats and hats from the coatrack and gives Sid his. Stu enters and pours himself a coffee, goes to his desk as Linda MacArthur, the assistant producer, enters. Passing Sid and Bernie, she cleans off the desk and preps it for Barry.

BERNIE Sure, why not?

SID Good, good, good . . .

BERNIE You know, Sid, it's gonna be a wet track.

SID 'Course it's gonna be a wet track. Been raining all day, how they gonna keep it dry? Wipe it off with a towel? . . . Can't be done!

BERNIE So who do you like in the third race?

SID We keep talkin' we're not gonna make it till the fifth. Did you see my car when you came in?

BERNIE No.

SID I was coming out of the Pick-N-Pay and there's this kid sitting on the hood of my car. And he's got circles, you know, around all the rust spots.

BERNIE What, a whacko?

Bernie and Sid exit.

SID (Offstage) No, a black kid. So he tells me for ninety-five dollars he can take out every ding and rust spot. I couldn't believe it . . .

The news and weather can be heard over the sound system as Linda and Stu get ready for their show. They work efficiently, hardly speaking. Linda cleans off Barry's desk, checks his mike and headset, puts out pencils and paper, and pours him a fresh cup of coffee. Linda's job during the show is to make sure Barry has everything he needs, to keep track of when commercials are aired, and generally to make sure the show is running smoothly. It is no coincidence that Linda is a very sexy blonde. Stu likewise cleans off Bernie's mess from his operator's desk, *whipping the garbage into a small trash basket next to Barry's desk. Stu's job is to field the phone calls that come in to Barry, screen them, and pass them on to Barry's desk. He also helps to cue Barry when a commercial is coming up. His job is something like an air traffic controller's. Stu looks over at Barry's desk, the empty chair. Lights a cigarette. Stu looks at his watch, takes a deep breath.*

STU Two minutes . . .

LINDA *(As she refreshes Stu's coffee)* I called my mother in New Jersey this morning. I told her the show was going national. . . . She wanted to know if that meant we were gonna be on TV! Isn't that a riot?

Barry Champlain enters. He's a wiry man who's moving a little too fast. He acts very sure of himself, but there's an edge.

BARRY *(Coming in the door past Spike)* Spike, how ya doin' tonight? Stu! *(Slaps hands with Stu, then launches into a story)* Hey, listen to this. Last night I call this Chinese restaurant. I'm ordering take out. I'm celebrating, figure it's the last time in my life I ever have to eat take-out Chinese food. I dial the phone wrong. I get this Chinese betting parlor. I'm talking on the phone to this Chinaman bookie. . . . Guy doesn't take bets on sports or horses, he takes bets on animals that fight each other. . . . Dog fights, pit bull fights, Chihuahua fights, poodle fights! Cockfights! Monkey fights! Frog fights! Frog fights, Stu! I put down some money, won a hundred bucks on a frog named Hung Far Low! *(Turns to Linda)* Linda, come on, let's go. We're wasting time!

Linda has been waiting with clippings in her hand.

LINDA You wanna hear these?
BARRY I'm here, am I here?

STU Sixty seconds to air, Bar.

Stu looks at his watch. Barry has seated himself at his desk during the inter-change, starts pushing buttons, sipping coffee, getting ready. Linda puts the clippings down in front of him and reads the headlines from her clipboard. Barry half-listens, makes little grunts after each item ("yeah," "uh-huh," etc.), flips through the clippings.

LINDA North American Boy-Love Association has a chapter in Shaker Heights. . . . They found a woman with sixty-seven cats in her house; she was raising them for their pelts! . . . A guy was arrested this morning; he had three women chained to the wall in his basement, said they were his "harem"—

STU Thirty seconds.

LINDA —Three out of four people say that they prefer watching—

BARRY *(Testing his mike)* Spike, beam me up, baby, beam me up!

LINDA Are you listening to this?

BARRY *(Patronizing)* I'm listening. I'm listening. Yeah?

Barry scrutinizes the clippings on his desk.

LINDA Three out of four people say that they prefer watching television over having sex with their spouse. . . . A guy in San Jose, California, wants to be a surrogate mother, says he can do it. . . . Report on AIDS—

BARRY I don't wanna talk about AIDS—

STU Fifteen.

LINDA OK . . . uh. . . . Homeless people are living in an abandoned meat packing plant in Willard. Some of them used to work there before it shut down—

BARRY Where's Willard?

LINDA Stu, you know where Willard is?

STU Here we go in five!

LINDA Dan called, said he'd drop by.

This interests Barry.

BARRY Why?

LINDA Guess he's nervous.

Linda exits.

BARRY I'll make him nervous . . .

As he says the words, the room fills with the chords of George Thorogood's "Bad to the Bone." A pretaped announcer's voice follows.

ANNOUNCER'S VOICE-OVER "And now from the heart of the Great Lakes, it's time for Cleveland's most popular and controversial talk show: 'Nighttalk' with Barry Champlain! And now, ladies and gentleman, here's Barry . . ."

Barry has taken a last sip of coffee, leans into the microphone. Stu points at him, and Barry picks up the beat perfectly.

BARRY Last night an eighty-year-old grandmother was knifed to death on Euclid Avenue, twenty people were watching, not one lifted a finger. Some kids need money for crack, so they stuck a knife in her throat. In Shaker Heights our good citizens . . . your doctors, your lawyers, your dentists . . . have formed a little club, they're having sex with children. . . . And on the West Side, fifteen churches were busted last week, for, get this, illegal gambling activities . . . and that's just in Cleveland!

This country, where culture means pornography and

slasher films, where ethics means payoffs, graft, and insider schemes, where integrity means lying, whoring, and intoxication . . . this country is in deep trouble, this country is rotten to the core. . . . And somebody better do something about it!

Tomorrow night, this show, "Nighttalk," begins national broadcasting. That is to say some smart guys at the Metroscan network have decided to pick us up for the benefit of people all over America. Two hundred and fifty-seven stations in the United States and Canada. How about that? How about that?

Some people have asked me if I'm gonna soften my touch on the national show. That's impossible. It can't be done. If I had to do that I might as well quit. This decadent country needs a loud voice, needs somebody to shake it up . . . and that somebody is me!

I have a job to do and I'm gonna do it . . . and I need your help. . . .

Now this is what I want you to do. . . . Are you listening? I want you to do something very simple. There's a thing in your house called a telephone. I want you to pick it up. . . . Go ahead, put your hand out and grab it, hold it up to your face, and dial 555-T-A-L-K. . . . Open your mouth and tell me what we're going to do about the mess this country's in!

This show goes national tomorrow night and that means the nation is listening. You better have something to say. . . . I know I do. (*Picks up his headset and puts it on as he speaks*) This is Barry Champlain, hold on to your radios. . . . Let's go to the first caller. Francine.

FRANCINE Yes, Barry.

BARRY How's your life tonight?

FRANCINE I have a little problem I'd like to discuss . . .

BARRY Shoot.

FRANCINE I'm a transvestite.

BARRY Uh-huh.

FRANCINE And I'm trying to save money for an operation—

BARRY Francine . . .

FRANCINE What?

BARRY This isn't interesting—

FRANCINE Let me finish what I was saying!

BARRY Francine . . . in your wildest imagination . . . what possible interest do you think your personal adventures in surgery would hold for my listeners?

FRANCINE I don't care about your listeners, it's something I *have* to talk about!

BARRY I don't. (*Cuts Francine off*) Nighttalk. . . . Yeah, Josh?

JOSH Thanks a lot, Barry. Uh, Barry, don't you think that the policies the World Bank is following only hurts the economies of Third World countries to the benefit of American banks?

BARRY Hold on! "Third World countries"! "Third World countries"! Where'd you learn that phrase, in college? Something you saw on "Sixty Minutes"?

JOSH It's a commonly used term—

BARRY Uh-huh. I hear it used all the time. It intrigues me. . . . You know what it means?

JOSH Of course I do.

BARRY Please tell us.

JOSH Well, it means developing countries . . . small poor countries.

BARRY Small countries . . . so India's not Third World?

JOSH Well, India is . . .

BARRY What about communist countries. . . . Red China, for instance?

JOSH No, not communist countries. . . . We're getting off the track. . . . What I was trying—

BARRY We're not getting off the track, Josh, we're getting on the track. The track is that you don't know what the hell you're talking about! You call me up and start spouting a bunch of left-wing mumbo jumbo about a subject you know nothing about! Yugoslavia is communist, it's a Third World country, so's Nicaragua, so's Cuba. Josh, go back to college and when you graduate gimme a call. (Cuts him off) Nighttalk, you're on.

JUNIOR Barry! Yeah, hey man, what do you think about the Indians this year?

BARRY In a word I'd say they suck.

JUNIOR Hey, I disagree with you on that one, Bar! They're gonna take the pennant. Niekro's gonna win twenty!

BARRY Are you nuts? Niekro's fifty years old!

JUNIOR Well, listen, you Mister Fuckin' Big Shot, Niekro has played better ball than any other—

BARRY Yeah. Yeah. Yeah. (Cuts him off) The Indians are gonna be watching the Series on the boob tube. Toronto will take the pennant, and the Astros will take the Series. On that deep note, let's break for a commercial.... This is "Nighttalk."

Barry pulls his headset off as Stu signals to Spike to begin running an ad.

STU This is a sixty, Barry.

BARRY Stu, let's cool it with the baseball calls tonight, all right? How's the board?

STU Board's good. Warming up. I got five hanging already... two look good...

Linda enters holding a bottle of Jack Daniel's and an empty glass. She is followed closely by Dan Woodruff, executive producer of "Nighttalk." He's a young businessman, nattily dressed.

DAN Barry! (Barry watches Linda pour him a stiff double) Just wanted to come by, say hello. (Nodding to Stu) Stu. We did it, Barry!

BARRY What do you mean, "we," Dan? You. You did it!

DAN You know what it is, Barry? They can't say no to ratings. That's the key. Do what you want, but get the ratings . . . then they can't say no. . . . You become an irresistible force.

BARRY Yup. Dan, we're in the middle of a show right now, gotta move it along—

STU Thirty seconds, Barry.

DAN I'm out. I'm out. "Genius at work." I know. . . . I'll leave you guys alone. (*Leaving*) Make it a hot show tonight!

BARRY It's always a hot show, Dan.

DAN Yeah, but tonight . . . *extra* hot. Don't wanna fuck this up. . . . We got a contract for six months, we want it for six years!

BARRY (*Friendly*) Sixty years! Six hundred years! Six thousand years!

Barry gives Dan a Nazi salute.

STU Six seconds.

DAN (*Laughing*) Sounds good. Sounds good. Oh, Barry, if you need anything, I'll be upstairs.

As Dan leaves, Barry settles in at his desk, waiting for the ad to wind down. Dan gives Linda a conspiratorial wink on his way out. Barry lights a cigarette, glances at his screen. Stu gives him a "go."

BARRY Ruth, you're on.

RUTH You're such a good man.

BARRY Hello.

RUTH You're so good, you care so much.

BARRY Hello, is this Ruth?

RUTH Yes, Ruth, this is Ruth. I was just listening to what you were saying, Barry, and you're so right! There is no more love, Barry. There is no more hope!

BARRY Well, I wasn't saying that exactly. I was saying that I can't help but wonder why—

RUTH No. No. You're right, Barry....Look at the world today. Hundreds of thousands of people starving in Africa.... And no one cares...that's all....They'll die.... And it can't be stopped, Barry. (*Barry, resigned to letting this one run a bit, finds his cigarette pack empty. He signals to Linda for a fresh pack. She comes over, disposes of the old pack, and leaves to get another.*) Who can stop the toxic wastes, the terrorism, the nuclear buildup, the starvation,...the assassinations? They tried to kill the Pope, Barry, what about that? You know, they killed Jack Kennedy!

BARRY Yeah, I think I remember reading about that somewhere....Listen, Ruth, you can't take the world's problems personally—

RUTH No, Barry, don't deny it. Don't act naive for our sake! You know the truth because you are an educated and wise man. And you're a courageous man to tell it. I'm so glad that your show will be finally heard all over this country because it's time that people started to listen to someone with a level head—

BARRY Especially people like you, huh, Ruth?

RUTH —the pollution is killing the trees, animals are becoming extinct. No more elephants, no more eagles, no more whales. Not to mention the rhinos, the condors, the grizzlies, the panda bears. No more panda bears!...What's the point, will someone tell me that?

Linda has entered with fresh cigarettes. She presses them into his hand.

BARRY Ruth, cheer up! Somehow the world will struggle on without the panda bears.... "Every cloud has a silver lining."

RUTH That's nice of you to say, Barry. But I know you don't believe it. You're just saying it to make all of us feel better. Because you are so good and kind. But, Barry, we don't deserve it . . . we don't deserve your love. It's our own fault . . . it's all our own fault . . .

BARRY Look, Ruth, the point is that I feel—

RUTH Thank you, Barry, for being such a good man. You are a prick in the conscience of the country. . . . If it weren't for you I don't know what I'd do. Take care of yourself. And good luck with your new show, we need it now more than ever.

BARRY Ruth, I was saying the point is that—(*A loud click is heard on the line; she's hung up*) I guess we've lost Ruth. . . . No more panda bears . . . no more Ruth! Gonna miss 'em. Hey, Stu, did she just call me a prick?

STU She called you a prick, Bar!

BARRY I think she called me a prick! . . . Makes you think. . . . What do you think? What do you say? Call me, I want to know. . . . "Nighttalk," Glenn, hello, you're on.

GLENN Hello, Barry?

BARRY You got 'im.

GLENN Oh. Phew. I never called before, I'm a little nervous . . .

BARRY That's all right. Relax. . . . Take your time . . .

GLENN Your show is great. You're great. I've been listening to you for a long time. . . . I used to listen to you when you were in Akron—

BARRY Goin' back to my hippie days.

GLENN Yeah. Heh. Heh. . . . You were great then too. Uh . . .

BARRY Yeah, OK. Thanks a lot, Glenn, what's on your mind tonight?

GLENN Well, something that woman was saying before about whales?

BARRY What about them?

GLENN Well, going extinct and, you know, the baby seals and everything . . .

BARRY Uh-huh. Ecology. Yeah?

GLENN Yeah...well, yeah, but what I was gonna say was more about animals in general, we should pay more attention to animals....We should give them more respect. I have a cat, Muffin,...and sometimes, uh, I live alone, and, uh, sometimes, I will come home from work and we, well, I make dinner, we have, uh, dinner together, you know?

BARRY You have dinner with your cat? At the table, you have dinner? What, with a tablecloth, candles, that kind of thing?

GLENN Well, no, heh-heh, of course not...

BARRY Oh.

GLENN She has her own plate. On the floor...

BARRY Oh, good!

GLENN But we'll eat the same things. Like if I have pork chops, she has pork chops...if I have a veal, she has a veal....And anyway, we spend time together....And sometimes I just think, that well, there are so many crazy, loud people in the world and then there's Muffin. Quiet. Not hurting anybody. Clean. Why can't people be more like that?

BARRY Lemme ask you something, Glenn. You and Muffin sound pretty intimate. You're not into anything funny, are you? She's fixed, isn't she?

GLENN Huh? Yeah, she's...hey, I don't like what you're saying about my cat!

BARRY There's a name for people who prefer animals over human beings, Glenn....I mean, Glenn, Muffin's fixed, maybe the way to get people to act like Muffin is to get them fixed? What do you think about that idea? Sound good? Snip off the old cojones?

GLENN No...that's not what I said at all! I don't think—

BARRY You don't think? You don't think? Maybe we should all get fixed. Then we'd be quiet like little kittens! Isn't that what you want, Glenn, huh?

GLENN No!

BARRY *What are we alive for, Glenn? We are not house cats!* Glenn, you got a choice, either start living, or go get fixed. . . . Take my advice, stop hanging around with the pussy and go find some! . . . "Nighttalk," Betty.

BETTY You think you're so smart!

BARRY Hello?

BETTY You're so smart, aren't ya? Cutting everyone off all the time. You know everything, don't ya?

BARRY Not everything, Betty. No one can know everything. Even I can't know everything!

BETTY Why are you always making fun of this country? Why are you always talking about drugs and niggers and Jews? Isn't there anything else to talk about?

BARRY You know what I hate, Betty? I hate people who call me up and tell me what they *don't* want to talk about. . . . If you don't want to talk about AIDS and *blacks* why do you bring them up in the first place? Huh? Sounds to me like you *like* talking about them. . . . If you don't want to talk about 'em then tell me what you wanna talk about or get off the phone!

BETTY Why don't you start telling the truth?

BARRY About what, Betty.?

BETTY You know what I'm talkin' about. . . . The people behind your show. . . . The people who pay the bills!

BARRY Lemme guess. You're talking about the sponsors now?

BETTY Don't act dumb with me. What kind of name is Champlain anyway? That's not a real name. You changed it, didn't you? Why? Maybe because it sounded a little too Jewish? Change the name, get a nose job . . . same old story. You think people are so stupid! No one's as smart as you are. . . . You think people never gonna find out about this propaganda that you and your bosses and the State of Israel are perpetrating on the American—

BARRY Wait a sec. . . . Hold on! State of Israel? *State of Israel!* Come on!

BETTY You know, there are two kinds of Jews—

BARRY Oh yeah?

BETTY —the quiet types and the big-mouthed types and you're one of the big-mouthed types . . . cut me off, I know you're gonna do it, go ahead!

BARRY I'm not going to cut you off, Betty. You're too interesting to cut off. . . . What you are saying reminds me of a little story . . . (*Pause. He looks at his drink, swirling it in his glass.*) Two years ago, I visited Germany, never had been there and wanted to take a look at Hitler's homeland. Are you familiar with Adolf Hitler, Betty?

BETTY I'm familiar with Hitler.

BARRY Good. . . . Now, although in fact, I'm not Jewish, I decided to visit what is left of a concentration camp on the outskirts of Munich. Dachau. You join a little tour group, go out by bus, everyone gets out at the gates. . . . It's rather chilling. A sign over the gate says: "Arbeit Macht Frei." It means "Work will make you free," something the Nazis told their prisoners. . . . Of course most of them never left. . . . Are you still listening, Betty?

BETTY I hear all your lies . . .

BARRY Good. I want to make sure you're not missing any of this. . . . Now, as I walked along the gravel path between what remained of the barracks, where the prisoners slept, and the gas chambers, where they died, I saw something glitter in among the stones of the gravel. I bent over to see what it was. What I had found was a tiny Star of David. Very old. Who knows, it might have belonged to one of the prisoners of the camp, perhaps a small boy torn from his parents as they were dragged off to the slaughterhouse. . . . I kept that Star of

David. . . . I know I shouldn't have, but I did. I keep it right here on my desk. I like to hold it sometimes. (*Swirling his glass of booze and studying it*) In fact . . . well, I am holding it right now. . . .

I hold it in my hand to give me courage . . . maybe a little of the courage that small boy had as he faced unspeakable evil can enter me as I face the trials in my own life . . . when I face the cowardly and the narrow-minded . . . the bitter, bigoted people who hide behind anonymous phone calls full of hatred and poisonous bile. . . . People who have no guts, no spine, so they lash out at the helpless. . . . The grotesquely ignorant people, like you, Betty, who make me puke. . . . People who have nothing better to do than desecrate history, perhaps . . . only to repeat it. . . . Are you still with me, Betty? (*Pause*) Betty!

BETTY Keep talkin', Jew boy. Life is short . . . (*Click*)

BARRY Uh-huh, Stu, let's send a microwave oven out to Betty. . . . "Nighttalk," Debbie, you're on.

DEBBIE Hello, Barry? Oh, I can't believe I'm actually on!

BARRY You're actually on. What's on your mind tonight, Debbie?

DEBBIE My boyfriend.

BARRY How old are you, Debbie?

DEBBIE I'm almost sixteen, Barry, and—

BARRY Goin' to school?

DEBBIE Yes, ummmm . . .

BARRY And your boyfriend, what's he, a senior or something?

DEBBIE He, uh, doesn't go to school, Barry . . .

BARRY Doesn't go to school, where's he work?

DEBBIE I don't see him all the time, so I don't really know . . .

BARRY You don't know whether your boyfriend works or not? That's interesting.

DEBBIE Well, see, the reason I don't know is that he leaves town sometimes and he kind of lives in his pickup truck. It's one of those that's all customized with tons of chrome on it. . . . He even has license plates that say "STAN-3" and everything and, ummmm, he tells me that he loves me, Barry, and I love him . . .

BARRY Uh-huh. Love is a hard thing to define. Fifteen, huh? Tell me something, Debbie, is he a nice guy?

DEBBIE Yes.

BARRY Well, you're a lucky girl to have a nice guy with a pickup truck in love with you. So what's the problem?

DEBBIE Well, see, I, um . . . (Quiet)

BARRY Debbie, hello? You still with us?

DEBBIE Yes . . . (Sniffing)

BARRY Debbie?

DEBBIE (Outburst) I'm going to have a baby, Barry . . . and now Stan isn't around. I'm going to have to tell my parents pretty soon . . . (Whimpering)

BARRY Now, now, hold on there, Deb. Nothing's that bad. You're pregnant. We used to call it "being in trouble." It's bad, but it's not the worst thing that could happen.

DEBBIE But my parents are gonna kill me, you don't understand!

BARRY Look at it this way, people have babies all the time. It's not the end of the world, it's the beginning! A little baby is coming! A little pink baby! Things could be worse, a lot worse. You could be sick, or dying. Stan could be driving around in his pickup truck and have a head-on collision, go through the windshield and die!

DEBBIE Barry, I want to die.

BARRY No you don't, young lady.

DEBBIE Yes I do!

BARRY No you don't, young lady! Now let's not start taking ourselves too seriously here.... You got yourself in a little trouble. You let your animal passions get out of hand and now the fiddler has to be paid, Debbie, right?

DEBBIE But, Barry, . . . he told me that—

BARRY Right? Am I right or am I wrong? Sounds to me like you want to blame the world for what you did. Well, don't expect a shoulder to cry on here, little girl, because you didn't think of these things in the wet heat of passion. You liked the feel of sex, you like the feel of being in love, you better like the feel of being pregnant.

DEBBIE (Crying)

BARRY Hey, now, no crying. Crying isn't going to fix anything. You're just gonna get the baby all upset. Debbie. Debbie. Now listen to me . . . is the baby kicking?

DEBBIE No of course not, I just found out! (Crying)

BARRY What?

DEBBIE I just barely found out!

BARRY (Laughing) Well, gee, the way you're going on there you sound like you're in labor! Come on! Snap out of it.... Debbie, can I ask you a serious question?

DEBBIE What?

BARRY Do you understand what has happened?

DEBBIE I wish I wasn't pregnant and I could go to school!

BARRY Yes, but, Debbie, are you sorry for what you've done? Debbie?

DEBBIE Huh?

BARRY Are you genuinely sorry for what you did to Stan?

DEBBIE Stan? But Stan did it to me!

BARRY But, Debbie.... You're not listening to me.... Now listen to me, Debbie!

DEBBIE What?

BARRY It takes two to tango! You seduced poor old Stan with your cute little fifteen-year-old body and now you want everybody to feel sorry for you! You did it so you could trap Stan into sticking around. Right? No wonder the guy can't find a job! Right?

DEBBIE Uh...

BARRY That's what I think happened. You think maybe that's what happened?

DEBBIE I don't know....I guess so...

BARRY Well then you have to deal with the consequences.

DEBBIE (*Pause*) So uh, then what should I do?

BARRY Do you know where Stan is?

DEBBIE No! (*Crying again*) I don't know where he is!

BARRY All right, all right, don't start crying again, spare me the crying....OK, Debbie, listen. This is what we're gonna do. We're gonna find Stan. Someone out there knows where he is, and I want them to call me here at the station....You leave your number with Stu and we're gonna call you as soon as we come up with something. And we will, don't worry. And let me say to anybody listening right now who knows where Stan is, you know, the guy who lives in the pickup truck, the one with all the chrome and the vanity plates that say "STAN-3."...Don't call the police....Give me a call at 216-555-T-A-L-K because we got a little girl here who's lookin' for her daddy....OK, Debbie?

DEBBIE Uh...yeah...I guess...

BARRY You're not gonna do anything crazy?

DEBBIE No.

BARRY Good. Stay warm, drink lots of milk, and stay away from the stuff under the sink and we'll talk in a little while....
A young lady with a problem. But here on "Nighttalk" every problem has a solution and that's why we're here. Let's go to a commercial. We'll be back with more...Nighttalk...

During the commercial, Barry pushes his chair back from his desk, rubs his face. Linda gets up and goes over to him.

LINDA You hungry?

Barry just points at his shoulders, and Linda comes up behind him and starts rubbing.

STU (*Has spun his chair to face Barry*) Hey, Barry, that guy talking about the old days in Akron. . . . It reminds me of that night that truck driver called who was stuck in his bathtub?
BARRY Oh, yeah! (*Laughing*)

Barry puts his feet up on his desk as Stu gets up to get a cookie from the coffee bar. Stu plays out the story to Barry's amusement.

STU Linda, this guy must have weighed four hundred and fifty pounds . . . stuck in the tub. What does Barry do? The guy doesn't want a rescue squad, so Barry calls up this massage parlor. Has 'em send over three hookers and a locksmith. And while these three bimbos baste this guy with joy jell, the locksmith's trying to pry him out with a crowbar! (*Barry's laughing now*) Great sound effects. . . . Guy popped when he came out—
BARRY Like a cork! Linda, you shoulda been there . . .
LINDA I'll get you a sandwich.
BARRY Four hundred pounds? No one weighs that much!
STU This guy did. . . . Ten seconds.

Linda is gone. Barry and Stu are getting back in the saddle.

BARRY That was in Akron?
STU Spring 'eighty-one . . .
BARRY Akron's ancient history . . . this is Cleveland.

STU You're on.

BARRY We're back. I'm Barry Champlain and you're listening to "Nighttalk." We got a pretty freewheeling show for you tonight. You call it, we'll talk about it. Your state of mind, the state of the union, whatever statements you wanna make, we're listenin'. Hello, Cathleen . . . you're on Nighttalk.

CATHLEEN Yes, am I on?

BARRY You're on!

CATHLEEN Boy oh boy . . . lots of good stuff to talk about tonight!

BARRY What's up, Cathleen?

CATHLEEN I loved what you were saying about your show going national and everything. It's important to say all that stuff—

BARRY Someone has to say it, Cathleen.

CATHLEEN I know, I know. I don't miss one of your shows because you tell it like it is, Barry. God bless ya! God bless ya. My best friend, Judy, she hates the show, she doesn't understand why I listen. . . . But to each his own, that's what I say. You tell it like it is and you've got guts—

BARRY I'm glad you feel that way—

CATHLEEN I have strong feelings and I don't hide them. Judy thinks your show is for nut jobs and psychos, but I don't agree. You say a lot of good stuff—

BARRY Yeah, Cathleen, I think you have to be more careful how you choose your friends.

CATHLEEN Yeah, I don't like her that much anyway—

BARRY She doesn't sound very likable—

CATHLEEN Only problem is, she's my only real friend.

BARRY Oh, yeah? I don't think someone who calls your beliefs "nutty and psycho" is a friend. . . . You got a real friend here, Cathleen—

CATHLEEN You're kidding me—

BARRY I don't kid when I'm talking about something serious like friendship. As your friend, I'm giving you good advice when I tell you to stay away from Judy...she's a bitter, cynical, pessimistic person...

CATHLEEN Maybe you're right.

BARRY Of course I'm right. Thanks for the call...(Cut off)... and we have Kent on the line....Hello, Kent.

KENT Uh, I need help.

BARRY Shoot.

KENT What?

BARRY Shoot. Shoot. Tell me what the problem is.

KENT Well...uh, I party a lot...you know, with my girlfriend—

BARRY How old are you, Kent?

KENT Eighteen.

BARRY How old is your girlfriend?

KENT She's sixteen.

BARRY All right, go ahead.

KENT So, we, uh...like to, uh, party, you know?

BARRY Kent. When you do all this partying, where are your parents?

KENT They go away a lot. Vacations.

BARRY Where are they right now?

KENT I don't know.

BARRY You don't know!

KENT They're on a vacation....Wait a minute, I remember...uh...Fiji. Is that right? Is there a place called Fiji?

BARRY Your parents are on vacation in a place called Fiji. So what are you up to? Partying?

KENT Yeah...except...well, that's what I wanted to ask you about...uh...we been partying for a couple a days...

BARRY A couple of days? What do you mean exactly when you say "partying"?

KENT You know, having sex...hanging around, eating, watching cable, getting high, listening to tapes...

BARRY Hold on. Back up a sec. Gettin' high? Smokin' pot?

KENT Well, yeah, we always smoke.

BARRY If you always smoke, what do you mean by "gettin' high"?

KENT Free-base. Smokin' coke. Crack.

BARRY Sounds pretty sordid....You've been smokin' crack for a couple of days...with your girlfriend....What else... you been doing?

KENT And drinkin'. And I dunno. I drank some Wild Turkey yesterday 'cause I was gettin' paranoid....Jill was doin' acid, I think. I'm not sure. Some Valiums.

BARRY You don't need to call me, Kent, you need to call a doctor and have your stomach pumped! Lemme give you a number to call—

KENT Yeah, but...see that's why I'm callin' you, Barry!

BARRY Why?

KENT Jill...she...uh, she's been sleepin' and uh...

BARRY (*Evenly*) No. No. No.

KENT She's been sleepin' and she won't, uh,...wake up, you know?

BARRY Don't waste my time with this baloney—

KENT Hey, she won't wake up! She's turning blue!

BARRY Oh, she's turning blue....You just tell Stu your address and we'll send—

KENT Hey, no, you gotta help my girlfriend!

BARRY Tell Stu where—

KENT No...that...I can't...I can't...(*Click*)

BARRY Hello! (*Shoots a look at Stu. Stu makes a throat-cutting gesture indicating that he hung up.*) Confusion reigns in Cleveland tonight....Let's break for a little commercial and we'll be back with . . . "Nighttalk." (*Stu signals to Spike, and sound cuts to upbeat station identification*) What's the problem tonight, Stu? You're throwing me some real curveballs, man.

Stu turns to face him.

STU What's wrong with curveballs, Bar?

BARRY Control, Stu, control! I don't need shit like that kid tonight! . . . Something on your mind? Something wrong at home?

STU No, Bar, there's nothing wrong at home—

BARRY Well then stay on the ball, all right? Give me the meat, not the poison.

STU (*Ignores Barry's mounting fury and turns back to his console*) You got it.

BARRY (*Jumps up and stalks over to Stu*) Stu, lemme see your board. Come on, run it! Who's this Henry guy, this nukes guy, you didn't gimme that! What about this Denise here, I didn't get that either. . . . What about the professor—

STU Barry, the professor is a stiff. All those people are stiffs. You want stiffs, I'll send you stiffs—

BARRY (*Interrupting him*) Stu . . . Stu . . . Stu . . . Stu . . . Stu, I don't want stiffs. (*Shouting now*) Am I speaking English? Read my lips. . . . Keep the show moving, gimme stuff I can work with! (*Practically screaming at Stu*) You having trouble understanding me tonight?

Barry goes back to his desk.

STU No, Barry, I'm not having trouble understanding you. In fact, I hear you loud and clear—

BARRY *Good!*

Barry slumps in his chair, turns away from the audience. Stu addresses the audience, turning in his chair, then standing and walking upstage center.

STU I met Barry Champlain in nineteen seventy-two. I was a DJ for a "progressive rock" station down in Akron and one day this guy shows up from Cambridge, Mass. . . . At least that's where he said he came from. . . . We were both hardass hippies . . . which meant of course that we were into subversive radio. . . . We thought we were changing the whole goddamn world right there in the studio 'cause we were playin' Lou Reed . . . and Frank Zappa or David Bowie. . . . Barry Champlain would . . . go beyond the tolerable. He'd play "Let It Bleed" twenty-five times in a row just for the effect . . . or find a record with a particularly good skip on it and just let it go. And I'd come by and we'd be hanging out, throwing down tequila and sucking limes, watching this record going round and round while the station manager is pounding on the studio door. . . . One time they had to knock the door down just to get Barry to take the record off. He didn't get fired, he got a raise. (*Laughs*) And the more I watched Barry the more I wondered why I was a DJ at all. I'd say things like "Here's the latest from Cream, it's called 'Wheels of Fire' and it's . . . really heavy . . ." Very embarrassing. Then Barry would get in the saddle to do his show and one second he's talking about his secret crush on Jane Fonda's breasts, next minute he's giving out the home phone number of every FBI agent in the state. . . . Then he started having people call in to the show. No one had done this in Akron before and I'm hanging out pretty much every day watching all this energy coming out of Barry. . . . And more and more people are calling in to the show 'cause Barry would say stuff like "Call me and tell me about your most intense orgasm . . ." and people would do it. He'd say: "Call me and tell me about your worst experience with a cop..." and they would be off to the races for the rest of the show.... He'd say, "Call me and tell me the one thing you've never told anybody else before in your entire life." One guy...one guy called up Barry and tells him that he fragged his lieutenant in Khesanh. He confessed it right on the radio. And he was cryin'. The guy wouldn't stop crying. Around that time Barry got his talk show here in Cleveland. I figured, to hell with being a DJ, I jumped ship and went with him. I listen to Barry Champlain take off for outer space every night, then the show's over and we go home. I mean, I go home to Cheryl and our kid.... Barry...I don't know what Barry Champlain does anymore.... It's not like the old days when we'd pick up a couple of girls and a fifth of Scotch and head for a room at the Holiday Inn.... Now he just splits, says he has to work on the show. And I can see him sitting at home making cups of coffee, chain-smoking cigarettes, and reading the fucking encyclopedia. Or worse. Maybe he just sits and waits to come back to the studio. He lost his voice once in nineteen eighty-three. Freaked him the fuck out. At first he was climbing the walls...then he started getting depressed.... Real depressed. I know what it was. He missed the sound of his own voice. You see, for Barry Champlain talking is like thinking out loud. That's why he loves radio. It's his life. He simply talks and all those people out there become part of him, part of his mind. I do too, I guess...

Lights back up on Barry at his desk, as Stu walks back to the console.

BARRY John, calling from Lorain.

JOHN Barry, hello, I'd like to comment if I may on what that lady was saying a few minutes before...the one who called you a Jew.

BARRY Yeah.

JOHN Well, I'm black—

BARRY Good for you. You wanna medal?

JOHN Heh-heh. No . . . I don't. No, don't play with me like them other people. I want you to know that I enjoy listening to your show and I have many friends who are Jewish—

BARRY How many?

JOHN Oh . . . three or four—

BARRY I wouldn't call that many—

JOHN They're very nice people, very educated—

BARRY Yeah, John, what's the point?

JOHN I like Jews and I think—

BARRY I don't know how to break this to you, John, but they're never gonna let you in the B'nai B'rith.

JOHN Heh-heh . . . that's not what I—

BARRY Hey, John . . . you're black . . . don't you know how Jews feel about blacks? They hate you. You know those slums over on the East Side where the rats eat little babies for breakfast? Jews own those slums. . . . What do you mean "I like Jews." What are you, some kind of Uncle Tom?

JOHN What the hell you know about Uncle Tom? I think you got your facts confused and I—

BARRY *I don't care what you think! No one does!* . . . You know why? 'Cause you're trying to kiss the master's butt, that's why! You call me up and try to get deep with me about how much you love Jews and you're lying. You hate them—

JOHN I don't kiss nobody's butt—

BARRY Sure you do! You kiss my butt. You're kissing it right now. If you weren't, you'd hang up on me!

JOHN That's what I'm trying to say, I don't want to hang up on you!

BARRY Then I'll do you the favor. (*Cut off*) "Nighttalk," Henry . . . you're on.

HENRY Yeah, hello, Barry—

BARRY Yessir.

HENRY Calling from Wheeling.

BARRY Long distance! How's the weather?

HENRY Good. Good. Um . . . I wanna talk about that nuclear power plant over on the river—

BARRY The Liberty Power Facility.

HENRY Yes.

BARRY I think it's a great idea. It's gonna cut our electric bills in half. You got a problem with that?

HENRY (*Clears throat, then monotone, as if reading*) "The Liberty Nuclear Power Facility is an infringement on the health and well-being of all the people living within a five-hundred-mile radius of its reactor core. We, the members of the Life and Liberty Alliance, protest the building, sale, or manufacture of—"

BARRY Wait a minute, wait a minute, hold on there one second, Henry—

HENRY "—nuclear and nuclear-related materials for any purpose, whether for armaments or so-called peaceful—"

BARRY Hey! Now shut up for a minute! Are you reading that? Stu, is he reading that?

HENRY "—utilization that endangers the life of millions of people in the Ohio River Valley."

BARRY Hey, shut up for a second. *Are . . . you . . . reading . . . that?*

HENRY That is our manifesto—

BARRY I don't care if it's the Magna Charta, you don't read anything over the air on this show. . . . Now, you got something to say, say it or you're off.

HENRY The use of nuclear energy is as irresponsible as nuclear war. We feel—

BARRY Oh, now it's nuclear war! Two minutes ago it was a power plant. How about toxic waste, that bothers you too, I bet. What about baby seals? Panda bears?

HENRY That has nothing to do with our protest—

BARRY Uh-huh.

HENRY We're talking about poison. We're all condemning ourselves with this nuclear doomsday machine. Our children . . .

They're talking over each other. Barry wins out.

BARRY Cut it, Henry, all right? What are you telling us? That we're all gonna die? I got news for you pal, we all die sooner or later. A nuclear war would probably be the best thing to ever happen to this country. Wake some people up.

HENRY I don't know how you can joke about nuclear war . . . this is—

BARRY Who says I'm joking, pal? Hey, I did my protest march bit back in the sixties. I been there, man. It was a lot of fun! I bet it's still a lot of fun. . . . *You don't care about anybody else, you just wanna go out there and have a good time!* Why don't you stop all this whining and start doing something more constructive with your time—

HENRY That's exactly what I am doing! I'm doing something constructive! Which is more—

BARRY Hold on, I'm not finished. You had your say, now lemme have mine. . . . You're just a spoiled, spineless little baby. You want to go crying to Mommy about what a nasty world this is, and then she'll fix it and make it all better. Put out that marijuana joint you're smoking, pal, and face the facts: Yes, a nuclear war is a very great possibility. And yes, Henry, it's scary. And, yes, we don't like it. But all the weepy pseudo-intellectuals in the world aren't going to change things one bit. . . . *(Pause)*

HENRY Your attitude is immoral.

BARRY Did I hurt your feelings, pal? Go tell it to your shrink—

HENRY WHEN THAT PLANT EXPLODES AND KILLS A FEW THOUSAND PEOPLE IT WILL BE ON YOUR HEAD!

Barry taunts him while he screams, finally cutting him off.

BARRY Too bad you can't keep up an intelligent conversation in a normal tone of voice. (*Cut off*) Bob . . . how's tricks?

BOB Barry, my friend.

BARRY Bob, what a relief. How you doing tonight?

BOB Terrific. Very well. Thank you. How are you?

BARRY Pretty well. Pretty well.

BOB Congratulations.

BARRY Thank you.

BOB I hope you're not gonna get too busy to take my calls.

BARRY Bob, no show is complete without your call.

BOB Hee-hee!

BARRY How are the legs?

BOB Oh they're fine. An ache or two, but not bad. You know what I say, "When they give you the lemons, make lemonade—"

BARRY You can't cry over spilt milk—

BOB Cry and you cry alone.

BARRY Because you can't lose what you never had.

BOB Because you don't know what you've got till you've lost it.

BARRY So don't lose hope, this too shall pass.

BOB Because today is the first day of the rest of your life.

BARRY Yeah, and it's always darkest before dawn. Bob, can I just—?

BOB Because tomorrow never comes—

BARRY Yeah, and if you play with fire you will get burnt. . . . Bob, can I say something, please?

BOB Of course, Barry.

BARRY Thank you. We are all inspired by your courage. You are a brave man and an example to all of us. As they say, Bob, the hero and coward both feel fear. The difference is that the coward runs away. You didn't run away. And we thank you for that.

BOB Well, thank you, Barry. But you know, people think that life in a wheelchair must be the worst thing in the world. That's not the way I look at it. I imagine the worst thing in the world would be being unthankful for all the good things that come our way every day: the smiles of little children, flowers blooming, little birds chirping, sitting on the budding branches on a bright spring day . . . hell! Just the sun coming up every day is a miracle!

BARRY I couldn't agree with you more, Bob, especially the part about the sun. . . . You know, I think we get too bogged down in our daily trouble, we forget about the simple things.

BOB Oh, I left out one more thing to be thankful for.

BARRY What's that?

BOB The Barry Champlain show.

BARRY (*Pause*) Thank you Bob, . . . us being both vets, it means a lot to me that you would say that.

BOB I mean it.

BARRY I know you do. . . . Look, we gotta move along, be well.

BOB Oh, no!

BARRY Sorry, gotta run. . . . I know you can't but we can.

BOB OK then. . . . And good luck with that kid . . .

BARRY Who?

BOB The one on drugs there? I hope he calls back.

BARRY Me too. . . . Look, Bob: Don't put all your eggs in one basket!

BOB And a bird in hand—

BARRY G'night Bob. (*Cuts him off*) And we have Denise on the line, hello, Denise—

DENISE I'm scared, Barry.

BARRY What are you scared of, babe?

DENISE Nothing specifically, but on the other hand . . . you know, it's like everywhere I go . . .

BARRY Yeah?

DENISE Well, like, Barry, you know, like we've got a garbage disposal in our sink in the kitchen, I mean my mother's kitchen . . .

BARRY Um-hmmm.

DENISE And sometimes a teaspoon will fall into the garbage disposal . . . (*As Denise continues to talk, Barry turns to Stu with a "what the hell is this?" gesture. Stu begs a cigarette. Barry, looking very sour, nudges the pack of cigarettes toward Stu, and he rolls over in his chair. Barry puts his hand over the mike and [inaudibly] asks Stu if he heard what he was saying five minutes ago. Stu says he asked for the call. Barry continues to listen to the call but gets more restless, finally cutting in on Denise.*) . . . ya, so like, you know how you feel when you have to reach down into that garbage disposal and you have to feel around down there for that teaspoon. You don't want to do it. Who knows what's down there? Could be garbage, a piece of something, so much stuff goes down there . . . or germs, which you can't see. You can't see germs, but if they're gonna be anywhere, they're gonna be down that disposal. They grow there, see? They come back up the pipes. Salmonella, yeast, cancer, even the common cold, who knows? But, Barry, even without all that, what if, and I'm just saying "what if," 'cause it would probably never happen, but what if the garbage disposal came on while your hand is down there?

BARRY (*Joking*) Boy, that would be a handful, wouldn't it?

DENISE I get so scared of thinking about it that I usually leave the teaspoon there. I don't even try to get it out. But then I'm afraid that my mother will get mad if she finds it down there, so I turn the disposal on, trying to make it go down the drain. But all it does is make a huge racket. And I stand in the middle of the kitchen and the spoon goes around and around and I get sort of paralyzed, you know? It makes a lot of noise, incredible noise. But Barry, I kind of like that noise, because I know the teaspoon is getting destroyed and annihilated and that's good 'cause I hate the teaspoon for scaring me like that—

BARRY Denise, Denise, Denise, Denise!...Lemme get this straight, you're afraid of the garbage disposal in your mother's kitchen?

DENISE Well it's not just the disposal, it's everything. What about insects? Termites. Hornets. Spiders. Ants. Centipedes. Mites. You can't even see the mites, they're like the germs. Tiny, impossible to see! I like things to be clean, you know. Dirty ashtrays bother me . . . (*Barry is fed up, shoots Stu a look [still sitting next to him], noticing for the first time that Dan is standing next to Spike in the control booth, watching Barry. When they meet eyes, Dan indicates that he wants to speak to Barry. Barry turns back to his microphone as Stu scurries back to his desk.*) . . . just one more unknown. Just like the houses on our street. Used to be we knew who lived on our street. But that was years ago. Now all kinds of people live on our street. Even foreigners, people with accents. What are they doing on our street? What are their habits? Are they clean? Are they sanitary?

BARRY Why don't you ask them?

DENISE Oh, sure, that would be a great idea just to go to somebody's house and just knock on the door. What if a serial murderer lived there? Ted Bundy? What if Ted Bundy or the Boston Strangler was just sitting inside watching television eating potato chips and I came to the door? Great! Come on in!

BARRY Wait a minute. Ted Bundy lives in your neighborhood, is that what you're saying?

DENISE I don't go to strange people's houses. I keep the doors locked at all times. I stopped driving, but that isn't going to solve anything. . . . You're not going to stop a plane from crashing into your house, now are you?

BARRY No.

Dan has entered onto the balcony, holds up one finger as if to say: "Just one minute, please."

DENISE The mailman brings me unsolicited mail and the postage stamp was licked by someone with AIDS. Right? My mother is a threat to my life just by persisting in going out there—

BARRY Out where? Where does your mother go?

DENISE Do you know that there's this dust storm in California that has these little fungus spores in it? And these spores get in people's lungs and it goes into their bloodstreams and grows inside them and kills them? Strange air . . . strange air . . . you have to. . . . Oh! There's my mother. I hear her key in the door. She'll kill me if she finds out I used the phone.

Denise hangs up. Click.

BARRY Strange air . . . that's what we've got for you tonight. I think I see my producer, Dan Woodruff, lurking in the corner warning me that if I don't wedge in a word here for our sponsors he's gonna do something outrageous, like remove his toupee. Don't wanna have that happen. . . . So lemme tell you where to eat . . .

Barry signals to Stu, and an ad gets thrown on (see Appendix). It runs under the following scene, audible as Dan exits.

DAN Barry—

BARRY Linda! Coffee please?

DAN Barry, I need your opinion on something—

BARRY (*Ignoring Dan*) Stu, check the level on line three, I'm getting a buzz there—

DAN Barry, I need ten seconds of your time—

BARRY What, Dan, what? I'm in the middle of a show here. I don't have time to chew the fat with you!

STU Thirty seconds . . .

DAN (*Has come down to stand next to Barry*) Barry, that kid who called, the one on drugs, with the girlfriend—

BARRY Kent, yeah?

DAN Kent . . . is a problem. We've got sponsors listening tonight, national sponsors. They just called and they're concerned about Kent. They think you should do something, say something.

BARRY What do they want me to say, Dan? It's a hoax. There's no girlfriend. I get calls like this all the time—

DAN They don't know that.

BARRY *Who* doesn't?

DAN (*Gently*) The sponsors, Barry. The people who are going to put you on the air coast to coast tomorrow night—

BARRY (*Jumping up*) Dan, all right! All right! (*Walks over to Stu*) Stu, chances are this kid Kent is gonna call again. When he does, shoot him to me and I'll talk him out. . . . Make you happy, Dan?

Barry stalks back to his desk, pissed.

DAN Thank you, Barry. I know you know what to do. . . . Oh . . . what if it isn't a hoax? What if the girl is dead?

BARRY We'll send her a wreath.

Dan exits.

STU Harry's Restaurant . . . runs long . . .

Barry is sitting at his desk, boiling. Harry's Restaurant ad is droning on. (Done as a "live spot," with Barry's voice prerecorded to sound live, very folksy. See Appendix for complete ad.) "And with that you get your choice of french fries, baked or delmonico potatoes. Choice of two vegetables. Cup of coffee or tea or soft drink with your meal. And . . . dessert from the dessert bar. . . . Lots of good things to choose from. Can you beat it for five ninety-five? I don't think so. . . . Harry's Restaurant for good solid food. You'll be happy to leave a tip . . . for your waitress . . . at Harry's Restaurant, I know I always do. I go there as often as I can. . . . Really excellent. . . . Tell 'em Barry sent you."

BARRY Wait a minute, before I take any more callers I have to say something. . . . Isn't that the most sickening ad copy you've ever heard? Harry's Restaurant? Home cooking? You ever go back into the kitchen of that place and you'd think you were in a taco stand in Tijuana! That was a pretaped commercial you just heard, everybody, something the *sponsors* force me to do. They like to make Barry sound homey and candid. Makes me wanna throw up. Which I usually do whenever I eat at Harry's. . . . "Nighttalk," Joe.

JOE Barry!

BARRY Yessir.

JOE I been drivin' cab for eleven years. . . . Last week I picked up a lady at the airport, rich bitch, you know what I'm saying? Wanted to know if I could take a check. . . . I said, "Lady, I'm a working man . . . gimme cash. . . . " She said she don't got it. I said, "Well, gimme that fancy watch a yours there and when you come up with the dough, I'll give it t'ya back. . . . She ran outta the cab.

BARRY She stiffed you.

JOE You're damned right, she did. 'Cause she's got rocks in her head. Like the jerks who call your show. What the hell's wrong with that kid who just called? The one with the girlfriend who OD'd?...He got a problem? What he needs is a good bust in the chops.

BARRY You're referring to Kent, the guy who likes to "party"?

JOE Yeah. Yeah. Kid like that needs some discipline.

BARRY You think that would do it, huh, Joe?

JOE Lemme tell you something, Barry. I got two kids and they gimme any trouble and I just take off my belt. They see the belt and that's it.

BARRY How old are your children, Joe?

JOE My little girl's five and my boy's three and a half.

BARRY You hit them with a belt?

JOE A brush, a belt, a newspaper. Whatever. The wife thinks I'm too hard on 'em. Hey...they're either gonna get it from me, or they're gonna get it out there.... (*Barry is getting seriously angry. He glowers at Stu for letting this call through.*) The world's a crazy place, Barry, filled with crazy people....You make a small mistake, you pay for it the rest of your life.

BARRY Tell me something, Joe. What was your mistake?

JOE Being at the wrong place at the wrong time.

BARRY You were set up?

JOE You could say that.

BARRY And let me guess, you went to jail.

JOE Did a dime.

BARRY Ten years. Must've been quite the wrong place.

JOE Armed robbery.

BARRY Tell me something, Joe, what's jail like?

JOE Waste of my time.

BARRY And you've got better things to do with your time.

JOE You better believe it.

BARRY Like beat your kids with brushes and belts.

JOE Huh?

BARRY You're the jerk. You're a child-molesting lunatic.

JOE Yeah. . . . And what are you? A faggot?

BARRY What are you, a prick?

JOE How about this? . . . I come down to the station right now, pal, and bust your faggot face in?

BARRY (*Starts laughing*) Who ya gonna get to help ya? Ya brother?

JOE Don't say nothin' about my brother!

BARRY Your brother's a creep and a pinhead just like you are. Your wife still sleepin' with him?

JOE The wife don't screw around. Don't get me angry.

BARRY What do you beat your wife with, Joe, a baseball bat?

JOE I'm coming down there . . .

BARRY Please . . . we're all waiting. . . . You want me to call you a cab? Oh, I forgot, you drive one!

JOE I know what you look like. I know where you live. You're dead. (*Click*)

Deadly pause. Barry is steaming.

BARRY "Nighttalk," June.

JUNE Hello?

BARRY Hello.

JUNE Hello? Am I on?

BARRY You're on.

JUNE Oh, Barry, I wanted to say something about the people who don't pick up after their doggies when they are walking them. . . . My Buttons is just a small poodle so all I have to take along is a little garden spade. I think some people would need a snow shovel.

BARRY Yeah, that's pretty disgusting, June.

JUNE It is disgusting . . . it really is . . . but, Barry . . . that young man who was having a drug overdose . . . is he going to die? Eh?

BARRY We all die someday, June.

JUNE I . . . hah . . . I never thought about it that way before. . . . Do you have a doggie, Barry?

BARRY I own no pets.

JUNE What's that?

BARRY I don't have a dog, a cat, a mouse, a goldfish, or a gerbil. I own no pets.

JUNE Oh, but you have to have a pet! How can you live without a pet, Barry, eh?

BARRY Well, I'll tell you, June, when I was a kid my father gave me a golden Lab for my tenth birthday. Beautiful dog . . . very friendly. All the kids loved her—

JUNE Oh, yes, they're lovely doggies . . . lovely . . .

BARRY We used to go on long walks through the woods. . . . Goldie, that was her name, Goldie—

JUNE Like Goldie Hawn . . . what a nice name!

BARRY Yeah, well, one day we were out walking in the woods. Beautiful autumn day. The leaves were just changing on the trees. We came out to this highway. Goldie saw a male German shepherd on the other side, didn't look where she was going . . . got hit dead on by a Greyhound tour bus doing around ninety—

JUNE Did she die?

BARRY Of course she died, June. She was dragged for around a quarter mile.

JUNE Awwwww!

BARRY I never could bring myself to get another dog after that. . . . You never know what might happen . . . to your dog. Especially the small ones, little poodles like yours. . . . Always getting their heads caught in slamming car doors . . . or falling down garbage disposals . . . or sometimes, when you're talking on the phone, they get all wrapped up in that plastic that comes with the dry cleaning. And they're barking and strangling to death and you can't hear them. . . . You know what I'm saying, June? (*Silence*) June? June? June? Guess she had to go walk her doggie. . . . (*Furious*)Listen to this . . .

Barry gives Stu the signal and whirls around in his chair, leaving his back to the audience. The lights dim to begin Linda's monologue. The audience can hear a snatch of the station ID Spike has just flipped on, a sweet woman's voice: "555-T-A-L-K . . . you'll be picked up when it's your turn to talk to Barry." The station sound dims, and Linda turns to face the audience.

LINDA One night, after the show, I stopped by the lunchroom. I was thirsty, I was gonna get a Coke out of the machine. Barry was there. Sitting at the crummy table under the crummy fluorescent light. I didn't know him. I had been working here two months and he had said three words to me the whole time. He was sitting there staring at this ashtray full of butts. Just sitting. I asked him if anything was wrong. . . . He looked up at me like he'd never seen me before. Like he didn't even know where he was. He said, "I'm outta cigarettes." I said, "There's a machine down the hall. I'll get you some. . . . " I mean, he coulda gotten the cigarettes himself, I know, but he seemed like he couldn't at that moment. . . . He looked at me again and said, "Linda. Can I go home with you tonight? Can I sleep with you?" Now, I've had a lot of guys come on to me in a lot of ways. I expected this Barry guy to have a smooth approach but this was unexpectedly unique. I didn't say yes. I didn't say no. We went to this diner he likes and I watched him eat a cheeseburger. He was talking about something, what was it? Euthanasia. I remember, because I thought, "This guy really knows how to sweet-talk a girl." And the whole time smoking cigarettes, looking around, tapping his fingers. . . . Of course, we ended up at my place. As I was getting us drinks, I said to myself, "Linda, you know you're gonna go to bed with this guy, so let's get the ball rolling." He was nervous, like he was gonna jump out of his skin, so I started giving him a shoulder massage. The next thing, we're on the floor and he's kissing me like he was in the middle of the ocean, trying to get on a life raft! I got us into the bedroom . . . and I go to the bathroom for two seconds to get myself together and anyway, when I get back to the bed, he's asleep, curled up in a ball. All that night, while he slept, he's throwing himself around, tossing and turning, grinding his teeth, clenching his fists. It was scary. Next morning, he's up before me. Comes out of the shower, he's a different guy. Says he never slept so well. Then he comes over to the bed and . . . we made love. . . . Since then, we've spent maybe a dozen nights together. . . . Lemme put it this way, Barry Champlain is a nice place to visit, but I wouldn't want to live there.

Lights back up on Barry on the phone.

BARRY And now a caller we've all been waiting to hear from. . . . Where are you calling from, sir?

STAN Calling from Fort Wayne—

BARRY Been doing a little driving in the pickup?

STAN Yeah, I guess you could say that—

BARRY I just did. So tell us something, Stan, what are you going to do about your girlfriend here in Cleveland? She tells us you're gonna be a daddy.

STAN I just heard. . . . I didn't know. How could I know? I just stopped by here at Al's, I was getting gas and a couple of beers . . . and, uh, he asked me if I had a girlfriend in Cleveland.

BARRY Yeah, well the question is, Are you gonna have a wife in Cleveland?

STAN Yeah, I guess that's the question.

BARRY Well, you know what I think?

STAN What?

BARRY I think you better get your ass up to Cleveland.

STAN Hey, I just got here. I been drivin' all night! You think you can get me to turn around?

BARRY Yes, I do. I have your make, model, and tags—

STAN No, hey—

BARRY Don't "hey" me, buddy. You know what you did. We're talking about a fifteen-year-old girl!

STAN I didn't know she was fifteen! Anyway, it's none of your damn business, bud!

BARRY Well, that's just too bad, isn't it, Stan? You know why? Because they don't let you keep your pickup truck when you go to prison. I hear they love rapists there. You better bring along a large jar of Vaseline—

STAN (Nervous) I ain't goin' to no jail. . . . That's crazy.

BARRY Stu, we still have the number of the Indiana State Troopers?

STAN No! Hey! What the hell you think you're trying to do?

BARRY This is what you're gonna do, Stan. You're gonna call Debbie, get in your truck, fill the tank, and start driving. I'll give you five hours.

STAN Shit! (Click)

BARRY And we have Rose on the line. Hello, Rose.

ROSE I'm so excited, this is my first time!

BARRY I'll be gentle.

ROSE (Laughing) I'm so happy for you, Barry, and I just wanted to call you and congratulate you on doing a very good job!

BARRY Well, thank you, dear. And how's your life?

ROSE Well, I don't know what I'd do without your show. I listen every night. . . . I am the mother of five children: Mike Junior, Cindy, Charlie, Robert, and Nancy. She's the baby, she'll be four next month. And of course, Skippy, our beagle.

BARRY That's good news, Rose. Tell me something, are they good kids?

ROSE They're wonderful kids, Barry. Mike just finished college . . . Robert was elected president of his class and Cindy wants to be a brain surgeon and/or marry Jon Bon Jovi as of last week.

BARRY Heh-heh. I'm impressed.

ROSE Barry, can I just say something?

BARRY Sure, Rose. Make it quick.

ROSE My husband, Mike Senior, died four years ago, he had an accident with the lawn mower and—

BARRY I'm sorry to hear that.

ROSE Well, yes, so things have been a little tough for all of us. . . . But the kids have been terrific.

BARRY They sound terrific. You sound terrific.

Barry is obviously bored by this call. He gets ready to cut Rose off.

ROSE They are terrific and I'm getting better all the time. . . . I get tired. . . . My job gets me tired at the end of the day, but then I come home and I turn on your show and presto, I'm a new woman—

BARRY Well, thank you, dear. It means a lot to me. Thanks for the call—

ROSE Barry?

BARRY Yup?

ROSE Sometimes you remind me of my late husband, who was very gentle and loving and a good man—

BARRY I'm sure he was.

ROSE Barry, Mike died around the time of his birthday . . . so his presents were never unwrapped. . . . I know this sounds . . . I feel almost silly saying this, but what's your shirt size, Barry?

BARRY Oh, well . . . heh-heh.

ROSE Everyone can use shirts. They're brand-new. They're just too nice to send to the Salvation Army! Silk shirts—

BARRY The station doesn't allow gifts. . . . I wish they would, but they don't. I can't accept any gifts—

ROSE I could deliver them personally. Gold cuff links—

BARRY Yeah, . . . uh, Rose, can I ask you a question?

ROSE You can ask me anything you want.

BARRY Well, you know I sit here every night alone in the studio happily chatting with people and I have no idea . . . I mean I can tell from your voice that you are a very, very attractive woman . . . and I was wondering, you know . . . (*Leans back in his chair, puts his feet up, and keeps talking*) I can see you at home right now, sitting in your kitchen . . . you've got the radio on there next to you and maybe a cup of coffee. Here we are talking on the phone, I've got my coffee and you've got yours. Two kindred souls sitting with our cups of coffee in the middle of the night. Alone together. . . . And I just, uh, was wondering what you were wearing . . .

ROSE Wearing?

BARRY You're wearing something?

ROSE Well, yes. . . . I'm wearing my bathrobe right now.

BARRY Uh-huh, sure. . . . You just got home from work. You put on your bathrobe. What sort of bathrobe is it, Rose?

ROSE Well, it's cotton and it has a sort of a blue print all over it . . .

BARRY (*Has become sultry and whispery*) Uh-huh. . . . Uh-huh. . . . Are you wearing slippers?

ROSE Yes.

BARRY Furry ones?

ROSE Yes.

BARRY Stockings?

ROSE No.

BARRY Panty hose?

ROSE (*Pause*) No.

BARRY Are you alone right now, Rose?

Rose's voice becomes halting. Barry eggs her on with soothing "uh-huhs" and "yeahs."

ROSE I am alone right now, Barry. I haven't been, uh, dating for a while, well, uh, not since Mike died and so it's a nice feeling to hear your voice . . . on the phone . . . right now. . . . It's nice to have someone special to talk to— (*Behind Rose we can hear children: "Mommy! Mommy!"*) Shhhhh! Please! I'm on the phone right now!

BARRY Gee, Rose, you told me you were alone. You just said you were alone, Rose!

ROSE I'm sorry, Barry, . . . uh, . . . should I send the shirts?

BARRY Well, when would you have the time, you sound so busy there. Listen, Rose, this is what you do. . . . Don't give those shirts to anyone else, save 'em for me, will you, please?

ROSE Of course!

BARRY And call me back in a month . . . make it two months, will you call me back in a couple of months, Rose?

ROSE Of course . . .

BARRY You promise you'll call me back?

Stu has hastily scribbled a note and passed it over to Barry during this exchange. Barry reads the note as he continues to talk to Rose.

ROSE I'll call you back in two months!

BARRY Good. Look, I got a very important commercial coming up, so I gotta move it along here, Rose, but I want to thank you very much for calling.

ROSE Thank you, Barry. I think—

Barry cuts her off.

BARRY What a lovely, lovely woman you are, Rose...and me? I'm Barry Champlain...and you, you're listening to Cleveland's most popular talk show, "Nighttalk." Gotta break for a little station ID here, but we'll be back...with more... "Nighttalk"! (*Turns to Stu. Theme music comes up.*) What do you think?

STU I think he's lyin'.

BARRY Lemme have 'im.

STU Here we go.

BARRY (*Back to his mike*) And we have Kent with us once again....Kent...

KENT I didn't mean to hang up on you.

BARRY But you did.

KENT Yeah...I...

BARRY Listen, Kent,...you're a fake. You're a hoax. You call me with some fake-o story about how you and your girlfriend are taking drugs and she's OD'd and your parents are in Acapulco—

KENT Fiji.

BARRY What?...Fiji...an important detail....And you're just this mixed-up kid who doesn't know what to do—

KENT It's true—

BARRY I don't believe you.

KENT Well, there's no way to prove it to you—

BARRY Sure there is, give Stu your address and we'll send somebody over there—

KENT No. Uh-uh. No way!

BARRY Kent.... What are you trying to tell me, that your girlfriend...what's her name?

KENT Uh, Jill.

BARRY OK, Jill. Jill has what...OD'd?

KENT I don't know....I can't get her to wake up—

BARRY Yeah. Yeah. OK, we heard that already, you were smokin' crack and she won't wake up....What you think, I was born yesterday? OK, OK, I'll go along with you...just for fun....Just for fun, is she breathing?

KENT I'll check...

BARRY Oh, I can't believe this....Stu, can you believe this? Why am I talking to this guy? I must have some kind of morbid curiosity. Some dark force compels me to listen to this garbage.

Dan Woodruff has entered the studio.

KENT Yeah, she's breathin'. I think. It's hard to tell.... There's some, like, foam coming out of her mouth—

BARRY *What?!*

KENT There's foam coming out of her mouth!

BARRY All right, all right....I've had enough of this baloney. You and I both know you're lying. I'm cutting you off...get off my show!

KENT No, wait!

BARRY That's it.

KENT Listen! My parents *are* in Fiji...but, uh,...the stuff about my girlfriend—

BARRY What?

KENT She...

BARRY Come on, Kent, spit it out!

BARRY You'll cut me off!

KENT I won't cut you off.

KENT You promise?

BARRY I promise I won't cut you off, Kent.

KENT (*Starts laughing*) I made the whole thing up!

BARRY (*Glances slightly over toward Dan*) Kent?

KENT What?

BARRY I lied. I'm cutting you off, you've wasted too much time for one night—

KENT *No! No! Please!*

BARRY You think you've been jerking me around and I knew from the minute I heard your voice you were lying.... Sayonara. Good-bye.

KENT Please! Please! I'm not lying now! l gotta talk to you . . . please!

BARRY Oh, yeah, and what are you gonna tell me now? That your mother just slit her wrists and she's bleeding to death? How about your father? What's he got, a shotgun in his mouth? Gonna blow his brains out? Who else is dead, Kent?

KENT No one's dead.

BARRY Come on, who's dead? Who's dead, Kent? Who's dead?

KENT No one's dead. You're making me nervous! I just wanna talk!

BARRY We're talkin'. You got two seconds, talk!

KENT I listen all the time. I think about what you say. You say such cool stuff and I, . . . uh, . . . wanted to meet you.

BARRY Now you are goofing on me. Cut it out. . . . You wanted to meet me? You can meet me anytime you want. I'm right here at the station.

KENT At the station?

BARRY I'm not the President, for God's sake. I'm right here. Downtown. In the Terminal Tower in the studio.

KENT I could just come down?

BARRY You could just come down—

KENT Now?

BARRY Now?

KENT Right now?

BARRY What do you mean, right now?

KENT Right now. Could I come down . . . and meet you?

BARRY I'm on the air, Kent.

KENT *Please!*

Barry looks over to Dan. Dan shakes his head no and emphasizes this with a gesture. Barry pauses, then:

BARRY Uh, sure, Kent, why not? Come on down. I'd love to meet you.

KENT Really? Really? Great!

BARRY Just hurry it up, we're already halfway through the show.

KENT Wait. Wait. Oh. I'll be right down. (Click)

Theme music comes over the sound system.

BARRY We're at the end of the first hour of exciting and intellectual conversation. Don't go away. . . . We have the news and the weather coming up and then we'll be back with more . . . "Nighttalk"!

His words are followed by a blast of theme music and station ID's, ads, and five minutes of the news, all of which runs under the following:

DAN Barry . . .

Barry gets up, walks past Dan to go to the coffee table. Stu checks his levels; once the news is on he leaves to go to the coffee room. Linda comes in.

BARRY Dan? Oh, you're still hanging around! Linda, go down and tell security this kid is coming....Dan, you want anything? Coffee, tea, insulin, crack? We have it all right here.

Linda starts to exit; Dan motions for her to stay. Barry pours himself some water, then turns to face Dan.

DAN Barry, you should ask me if you want to have guests on the show.

BARRY Why?

DAN Because I'm the producer, Barry, that's why.

BARRY Dan, you asked me to talk to him and I did.

DAN Well, he's not coming on the show. That's it. There's too much riding on what's happening tonight.

BARRY What's happening tonight, Dan?

DAN I told you, the sponsors are listening tonight. Ralston Purina, the dog food people!

BARRY Dan, this is my show. The sponsors bought my show. If I want to have this kid on my show, I'll have him on the show. I put who I want on my show....If I want to have Charlie Manson on my show, I'll have him on. Or Ted Bundy, or John Wayne Gacy...or Sirhan Sirhan.... *(He's on a tear)* Or how about this, Dan? I get David Berkowitz, Bernhard Goetz, and John Hinckley on, and we do a special on gun control! Or wait...even better, we can get a few of those guys who go into shopping centers with automatic weapons, M-16s.... *(Turning to Linda)* What was the name of that guy in San Diego, McDonald's?

LINDA Huberty?

BARRY That's it! Huberty, James Huberty! We get James Huberty and we get the Texas tower guy, Charles Whitman... make a great show, Dan. Dan, you gotta think about these things, 'cause you're the producer.... (*Turning to Linda*) Whatever happened to Richard Speck? And the nurses? Let's bring them on the show! *Wayne Williams*... bring him up from Atlanta! Look, Dan, I gotta take a piss, gotta get going.... (*Starts to exit, from the balcony*) Wait! I got it! Whatever happened to that postman from Oklahoma? He killed fourteen people, Dan. *He killed his boss!* We bring him on the show.... Bring *you* on as a special guest! (*As he exits*) That's it, that's what we gotta do.

Linda has found this amusing. She looks at Dan, who just glares. She exits.

DAN (*Addresses the audience*) Mantovani...Bacharach...Mancini...the Living Strings...the Jackie Gleason Orchestra.... The name for it is "easy listening,"..."beautiful music," ...gentle,...serene,...melodic,...reassuring. The kind of shit you hear on elevators. The kind of shit this station played between nineteen sixty and nineteen eighty. Mindless. Insipid. Disturbing. They hired me in 'eighty-one because their easy listening format was losing the battle against the Rolling Stones and Grand Funk Railroad. I told them I wanted to put together something new: an all-talk station. I wanted to grab all the top talk talent in the Midwest and create a team that would be unbeatable. That was my idea, an all-talk station. I told them take it or leave it. They took it and I got myself the best sports commentator, a financial whiz, a psychologist, a home handyman specialist, and a sweet old guy that old ladies just loved to chat with. I had myself a full deck...but I was missing the joker.... Then I heard Barry Champlain. He was down in Akron. A crazy DJ who liked to take callers. Liked to get people wound up....I also heard he was a pretty self-involved guy. Figured. "Champlain." His real name was Paleologus! I went down to see him. Had lunch. Told him my plan. I looked over his resume, saw that he had been stationed at Fort Dix for six months in 1969, got discharged for a hernia or something like that. So I turned him into a Vietnam vet. I asked him if he ever smoked pot. He said he did maybe once or twice, so I turned him into a hippie too. Barry Champlain marched in all the antiwar marches... after he saw the horrors of war in Southeast Asia, of course. He also knew how to fly a plane, lived in a tent in the Yukon for a year, and pitched minor-league baseball for the Toledo Mudhens.... Oh, yeah, I'm particularly proud of this one: He got a Ph.D. in history at the University of Chicago after writing a book on Martin Luther and the Reformation. A Renaissance man.... Barry just sat there chewing his tuna fish sandwich, staring at me.... The gears were turning in his head. Then I hit him with the zinger... the name of the show: "Nighttalk with Barry Champlain." His name would be *part* of the name of the show.... He stopped chewing.... I had my joker. (*Stu and Spike resume their places in the studio*) Talent comes and goes. Like trains in and out of the train station. Trains wear out, they get derailed, they crash. Sooner or later, they're out of commission. The faster they go, the harder they crash.... Barry's my train. (*Barry enters, rushed, puffing on a cigarette. He goes directly to his place, not seeing Dan.*) I put him on the track. I keep him on the track. I keep him oiled and on the track. I let him go as fast as he can. The faster the better. (*As he leaves*) This is a great job. It's fun, I enjoy myself every day. And it's a challenge.... And you make a pretty good buck.... I'd say it's just about perfect.... You get into trouble when you forget it's a job. When you start to think you're doing something more.... It'll fuck you up every time. Every time. That's Barry's problem, not mine.

Dan exits.

BARRY *(Resumes taking calls)* "Nighttalk," Vincent.

VINCENT I been listening to you for five years—

BARRY Yeah?

VINCENT Yeah, the guys here at the store put you on every night. We sit around and laugh at you cause you're a jerk-off and a loser—

BARRY *(Cuts him off)* Nighttalk, Agnes?

AGNES Barry, can I ask you a question?

BARRY Hit me, babe . . .

AGNES Oh, I wouldn't hit you for the world! "I Love Lucy" . . . Why don't they make more of 'em?

BARRY What?

AGNES The "I Love Lucy" show. It's so good, why don't they make more of them? I feel like I've seen each one at least ten times! It's time to make some new ones—

BARRY Those shows are ancient, Agnes! Lucille Ball is an old woman and the rest of the cast is dead!

AGNES No, she's not that old. I saw her on the show the other night, she looked to be around thirty-five! And that Ricky Ricardo, boy can he play the bongos—

BARRY *No one can be this stupid!* Are you serious, Agnes? Do you know what year this is? *(Cuts her off)* Nighttalk, Chris!

CHRIS Good evening, Barry.

BARRY Yeah?

CHRIS Some people think God is dead. Do you think God is dead, Barry?

BARRY I happen to know that God is alive and well and living in Gary, Indiana. He's a black steelworker with seven kids who works the night shift pouring off slag.

CHRIS I see. But, Barry, do you believe in God?

BARRY What?

CHRIS Do you believe in God?

BARRY Are we being serious here, Chris?

CHRIS I'm serious. I think it's very important.

BARRY Why is it very important what I believe? Can't you think for yourself?.

CHRIS Don't you think that without some kind of belief in God our actions in this world are meaningless? It would just be physics and chemicals without God . . . just shapes and colors . . .

BARRY Shapes and colors? Come on! Chris! We been reading William Blake?

CHRIS I think you do believe in God.

BARRY Oh, you do?

CHRIS Yes, you believe in God.

BARRY Really? What makes you so sure?

CHRIS It's simple. You think you *are* God. And aren't you ashamed?

Kent is being led by Linda and is visible through the studio glass. As soon as Linda sees Barry's off-air she brings Kent in through the door.

BARRY (Pause, sideways glance at Stu) On that note, let's hear from our sponsors. Hope you stick around for the Second Coming. (Turns on Stu, furious) What are you doing to me, Stu? You're killing me, you're killing me right on the air. . . . (Sees Kent. Kent is standing there, shag haircut, torn jeans, tie-dye T-shirt—suburban deadhead—soaking up the ambience of the studio. He's amazed and proud that he's actually here.) Wait, don't tell me, I can guess . . .

LINDA He seems harmless . . .

Linda brings Kent to Barry's desk.

BARRY (*Glares at Stu*) Harmless as a baboon.

LINDA You'll sit over here, Kent. This is your microphone. Speak directly into it, keeping your mouth about six inches away.... Remember the ground rules: no phone numbers, no brand names, no last names over the air.... Otherwise, act and speak normally.... This is Mr. Champlain ...

KENT This is great! You're Barry?

BARRY You got 'im.

KENT Wow ...

Kent just stares at Barry.

BARRY What's wrong with him?

LINDA I think he's star struck.

Linda returns to her seat.

STU We're going in five ... four ... three ...

BARRY Come on, pal, ... we're on.

STU You're on with the kid.

BARRY (*Swings back into the show*) We're back. With me right now is a very special guest.... Kent.... Say hi to everyone, Kent.

KENT Wow ...

BARRY My sentiments exactly. We've brought Kent on board to give us an inside look at the future of America. Kent is the classic American youth: energetic and resourceful ... spoiled, perverse, and disturbed.... Would you say that's an accurate description, Kent?

KENT Yeah, sure ...

BARRY What do you call that haircut?

KENT Uh ... I dunno ... rock and roll ...

BARRY Are you high right now, Kent?

KENT High?

BARRY Are you on drugs? Or is this just your naturally moronic self? Wipe the drool off your mouth, you're getting the desk all wet.

KENT I can't believe I'm.... Does this work?

Kent speaks into the mike.

BARRY This is a radio station, Kent. You're sitting in front of a live mike.... When you speak, thousands of people hear your voice. It penetrates their minds.

KENT (*Screams a rock howl*) Wanna send that one out to Diamond Dave and Billy the bass player and all the babes at the mall—

BARRY Kent, we're discussing America here tonight. You have any thoughts on that subject?

BARRY America...is a country...

BARRY That's a good start.

KENT It's where the revolution was.... It's the home of democracy, like you were saying before...

BARRY Yeah, go on...uh-huh.

KENT That's how come we can have, you know, talk shows and TV and stuff. There's freedom in America. I wouldn't wanna live in Russia. You know, because they don't have freedom. And their TV shows suck. I think all they have is news.... I mean, the news sucks here too. All they ever talk about is Nicaragua and Iran. All these boring places filled with boring people. Who cares, you know? How come they never talk about cool places like London or Lauderdale or Antarctica...

BARRY Or Fiji? How about Fiji? You forgot Fiji, Kent.

KENT Yeah...yeah...

Kent spaces out.

BARRY Oh, I'm sorry, I broke your train of thought. Keep going, this is exhilarating.

KENT Well. . . . Nobody talks about what the kids are doing. I mean, it's not like I'm not into political stuff. The Live Aid concert was pretty good, you know. Hands Across America. I dunno. I like Bruce. And he's political.

BARRY Bruce? Bruce Springsteen. I hear he's a communist.

KENT Naw, he's from New Jersey. His babe's supposed to be pretty nice—

BARRY Whose babe?

KENT Bruce's!

BARRY Oh, Bruce Springsteen's wife. Yes, what about her?

KENT Julianne. She was a model. All the rock stars go with models. Keith and Patti. Mick and Jerry. Prince. I guess that's the way it works out. . . . The models hang around with the guys they think are the coolest and they want to make it with them. The stars.

BARRY Oh, really?

KENT You know what I'm talking about, Barry. Look at you, big star, famous guy . . . you've got that fine fox right over there that works for you. (*Flips his tongue at Linda*) Models. So, if you've got some cash, and you're cool, you get to have a model . . .

BARRY So you're not into women's liberation?

KENT Yeah, I am. I'm into everybody being liberated. Women, South Africans, all those kind of people. I saw a show about all that stuff. . . . Revolution is pretty important, you know? There's gonna be a lot more revolutions. When the people get together, solidarity, you know? Like that song by MegaDeath (*Singing and pounding on the desk*) "Peace sells, but who's buying?" Plus . . . plus I saw a show about how people will have two-way televisions so they can see each other and then they won't be able to stop the revolution—

BARRY Who won't be able to stop it?

KENT Big Brother . . . the government. . . . They're all a bunch of fascists, they wanna control everybody's mind. But freedom's an important thing. Like you always say. You say the best things, Barry. I listen to you all the time. You're great.

BARRY Swell, Kent, and I mean that from my heart. So you just felt like calling tonight and making my life miserable? You got thousands of people worried about your girlfriend, Jill . . .

KENT Yeah, I guess I shouldna done that . . .

BARRY Is Jill dead, Kent?

KENT Nah. She's listening to the show right now. She's taping it.

BARRY For posterity I'm sure. (*Pause*) Kent, you're an idiot. . . . I sincerely hope that you don't represent the future of this country, 'cause if you do, we are in sad shape.

KENT Barry, . . . you're so funny! That's why I love to listen to ya show. . . . All the kids listen. . . . You're the best thing on the radio—

BARRY Kent, America is waiting for you and your friends . . . indeed the world is. . . . The future looks difficult in this country and in the world at large. . . . What are you planning to do about the armaments race, toxic wastes, organized crime, the breakdown of the political system? How are you going to prepare for the future?

KENT By listening to your show, Barry!

BARRY That's pretty funny. You're a funny guy, like to party, have fun. . . . Am I part of your good time?

KENT Sure.

BARRY Kent, we discuss a lot of disturbing subjects on this show. Tragic things. Frightening things. Doesn't any of that bother you?

KENT No.

BARRY Why not?

KENT It's just a show!

BARRY It's just one big rock video, huh?

KENT Yeah, Barry, you know . . . it's *your* show!

BARRY Yeah . . . that it is . . . that it is . . . my show. Let's get back to the callers on my show.

KENT Sure thing, Barry!

BARRY Julia.

JULIA Barry, hello, yes . . . I think . . . these people who have been calling you tonight are a bunch of I-don't-know-whats! It's crazy. And that crazy kid you got on there . . . that's terrible. I've been listening to you for five years straight, Barry, and I love you and your show. I think it's terrific that more people are gonna be listening. I just hope you have time for your longtime friends—

BARRY I always have time for my friends, Julia.

JULIA Your show's terrific. You're terrific and I don't know what else to say . . .

BARRY Well, tell me something, Julia, since you listen all the time, what is it that you like about the show?

JULIA Well . . . I don't know . . . a lot of things . . .

BARRY Well, what? For instance . . .

JULIA Well, I love you, Barry . . .

BARRY Yeah. That's a given. . . . OK, what about me do you love?

JULIA Well, you're very funny . . .

BARRY Uh-huh . . .

JULIA And I love to hear you talk about all the things you have to say!

BARRY OK, OK, well, let's get back to the show . . . the show must serve some kind of purpose for you . . .

JULIA Now, I wouldn't say that . . .

BARRY What would you say?

JULIA Well, I don't know? I . . .

BARRY What do you mean, you don't know? You've said that at least five times now! What don't you know? You been listening to this show for five years and you don't know why you listen to it?

JULIA I just said—

BARRY I heard what you said, you said you don't know why you listen! Why don't I tell you why? You listen to this show so that you can feel superior to the other losers who call in!

BARRY Barry!

BARRY Don't "Barry" me! You've got sawdust between your ears instead of brains. Just listen to you. If I sounded as stupid as you did, I'd be too embarrassed to open my mouth!

JULIA I'm hanging up!

BARRY Good. And don't call back.

She hangs up. Barry is silent. Pause.

KENT Wow.

BARRY "Nighttalk." You're on.

CALLER I just have one thing to ask you, Barry . . .

BARRY Hit me.

CALLER Are you as ugly looking as you sound?

BARRY Uglier.

CALLER Yeah, I thought you'd say something like that. But as usual you avoid the question . . .

BARRY *(Pause)* What's the question?

CALLER I think you know the question.

BARRY Is it animal, vegetable, or mineral?

CALLER The question is obvious, why does an intelligent fellow like yourself spend so much energy hurting other people? Do you not love yourself?

BARRY People who love themselves are in love with a fool.

CALLER Well put. Good night, Barry. (Click)

BARRY (*Stares at his microphone. He's feeling trapped.*) "Nighttalk." Allan.

ALLAN You love to cut people off, Champlain. You wanna push folks around, you know why? 'Cause you're a lonely, sorry mother...you're a failure. That jerk kid is making a jackass out of you—

BARRY (*Cut off*) "Nighttalk," Ralph.

RALPH They asked me, why did you do it? Why are you so angry?...They don't understand, Barry, me and you, Barry, we're the kind of people we feel too much—

BARRY Hey, Ralph, you playing with a full deck or what?

RALPH I'm not saying I have the answers, who does? I used to think I knew, but now, who knows? Take for instance, take cancer. What is it? A virus? A bacteria? What difference does it make? It kills you just the same...just as fast. I never saw an atom bomb explode, never did....The guys who did, they're dead....All we got is movies and the guys who made the movies, where are they? They tell me the little babies in Africa are starving....OK, I'll buy that...but where? Exactly where? And what am I supposed to do about it? See, all I know is me...and me, I'm gettin' screwed....Barry, they say that they're gonna come here and take my TV set and take my refrigerator....What are they gonna do with my TV set?

BARRY Probably watch it. That's what people do with TV sets.

RALPH But when they do, what do they see? They see people killing people, babies starving. Floods. And for what? For nothing. Beer commercials. Tampax ads. MTV. A yacht in the ocean. A diamond earring. A racehorse. I guess so. All I know is what I read in the papers. And that's a lot of talk-talk-talk-talk-talk—

BARRY Ralph, Ralph, Ralph, Ralph, Ralph...tell me something, I'm curious, how do you dial the phone with a strait-jacket on?

RALPH Sure, I'll listen, I'll listen to common sense. But who's got it anymore? Barry, even if you got it, you're the only one . . . just you and me. Nobody else. Everybody knows God is dead. You know why?

BARRY (*Subdued*) Why?

RALPH 'Cause God said he would destroy Sodom and he did 'cause you know why?

BARRY Why?

RALPH 'Cause Lot couldn't keep the Sodomites away from the angels. . . . They were trying to do it with the angels. . . . Lot tried to tell 'em, don't do it . . . but they wouldn't listen. And now the guy's dead. See what I'm sayin'? (*Barry has had enough, he's fed up. Pulls himself together to make a final assault on Ralph.*) I don't know much about God, I never was very religious, but you can't help feeling like something's wrong, like no one's drivin' the train . . . the system. Too many people gettin' sick and the traffic is always jammin' up and even the weather's not been very good lately. I don't get it, Barry, I don't—

Barry whirls toward the microphone, mouth open. But another voice is talking; it's Kent, shouting into his mike.

KENT You don't get it, wimp? Here's what you get: You get a dollar fifty-nine, go down to the drugstore, buy a pack of razor blades, and slash your fucking wrists, pinhead!

Kent is proud of his Barryism, while Barry's mouth is agape; he's unable to believe what is happening on his show.

BARRY (*Pause*) Let's hear from our sponsors. (*Whirls at Linda, unaware that Dan has entered during Kent's interview*) Linda! Get Kent a drink of water or something.

Linda gets up and starts moving toward Kent.

BARRY (*Under his breath*) Get him out of here, now.
LINDA Come on, Kent.

Linda starts leading Kent out.

KENT Hey! Barry!

Kent whirls around. He has something in his hand. He points it at Barry. A gun? No, a small flash camera. He flashes Barry, a few feet from his face. Barry is standing, temporarily blinded. Kent bounds out of the studio, past Stu, with Linda in pursuit. As Kent passes Dan, he flashes him as well. Barry steadies himself at his desk.

STU Thirty seconds, Bar.

Dan is standing on the balcony, smiling at the floor with patient embarrassment.

DAN Barry, I gotta say it.... You dispelled any doubts I had.... I loved it! Great choice, great work. Unorthodox show, but... interesting.... See you tomorrow, champ. ... Stu.

Dan turns to leave.

BARRY Dan! Where are you going?
DAN You don't need me here anymore tonight. See you tomorrow.
BARRY Dan! (*Sitting down in his chair*) What would happen if I don't come in tomorrow night?
DAN Huh?... Oh, well, I think they're holding your slot back in Akron, Barry... if you want it!

Dan winks and leaves. Barry stares at his microphone, a crooked smile on his face.

STU Ten seconds, Barry.

BARRY Fuckit.

STU Spike, pop me an ID, we need time here.

Stu is looking at Barry for a cue.

BARRY *(Snaps out of it, looks at Stu)* What are you staring at?

STU Tell the truth, Barry, I was thinking maybe we should send Linda out to pick up a bottle for after the show. Whaddyou say?

BARRY Show's a washout, Stu!

STU So we'll hash it out over at the Red Coach. . . . *(Pause)* C'mon, Barry, it's not that important, it's just one show.

BARRY If it's not that important, Stu, why am I doing it?

STU You don't like the heights, Barry, don't climb the mountains.

BARRY Fuck you.

STU No, not fuck me, fuck you. It's like the kid said, it's your show . . .

BARRY *(Can't argue)* Hold the calls. *(Stu points the "go" finger. Barry with bemusement turning to shouting anger into the mike.)* I'm here, I'm here every night, I come up here every night. This is my job, this is what I do for a living. I come up here and I do the best I can. I give you the best I can. I can't do better than this. I can't. I'm only a human being up here. I'm not God, . . . uh, . . . a lot of you out there are not. . . . I may not be the most popular guy in the world. That's not the point. I really don't care what you think about me. I mean, who the hell are you anyways? You . . . "audience." . . . You call me up and you try to tell me things about myself. . . . You don't know me. You don't know anything about me. You've never seen me.... You don't know what I look like. You don't know who I am, what I want, what I like, what I don't like in this world. I'm just a voice. A voice in the wilderness.... And you...like a pack of baying wolves descend on me, 'cause you can't stand facing what it is you are and what you've made.... Yes, the world is a terrible place! Yes, cancer and garbage disposals will get you! Yes, a war is coming. Yes, the world is shot to hell and you're all goners.... Everything's screwed up and you like it that way, don't you? You're fascinated by the gory details.... You're mesmerized by your own fear! You revel in floods and car accidents and unstoppable diseases.... You're happiest when others are in pain! And that's where I come in, isn't it?...I'm here to lead you by the hand through the dark forest of your own hatred and anger and humiliation....I'm providing a public service! You're so scared! You're like the little child under the covers. You're afraid of the boogeyman, but you can't live without him. Your fear, your own lives have become your entertainment! Tomorrow night, millions of people are going to be listening to this show, *and you have nothing to talk about!* Marvelous technology is at our disposal and instead of reaching up for new heights, we try to see how far down we can go... how deep into the muck we can immerse ourselves! What do you wanna talk about? Baseball scores? Your pet? Orgasms? You're pathetic. I despise each and every one of you.... You've got nothing. Nothing. Absolutely nothing. No brains. No power. No future. No hope. No God. The only thing you believe in is me. What are you if you don't have me? I'm not afraid, see. I come up here every night and I make my case, I make my point....I say what I believe in. I have to, I have no choice, you frighten me! I come up here every night and I tear into you, I abuse you, I insult you...and you just keep calling.

Why do you keep coming back, what's wrong with you? I don't want to hear any more, I've had enough. Stop talking. Don't call anymore! Go away! Bunch of yellow-bellied, spineless, bigoted, quivering, drunken, insomniatic, paranoid, disgusting, perverted, voyeuristic little obscene phone callers. That's what you are. Well, to hell with ya.... I don't need your fear and your stupidity. You don't get it.... It's wasted on you. Pearls before swine.... *(Catches his breath)* If one person out there had any idea what I'm talking about... *(Suddenly starts taking callers again)* Fred, you're on!

FRED Oh... hello... yes... well... you   see,... Barry,... I know it's depressing that so many people don't understand that you're just joking—

BARRY *(Cut off)* Jackie, you're on!

JACKIE I've been listening for many years, and I find you a warm and intelligent voice in the—

BARRY *(Cut off)* Debbie, you're on!

DEBBIE Stan called.... He told me that he never wants to see me again!

BARRY *(Cut off)* Arnold...

ARNOLD What you were saying before about loneliness, I'm an electrical engineer—

BARRY Lucy!

LUCY Barry, my mother is from Akron and she wants to know if you went to high school with—

BARRY Larry!

LARRY Why do people insist on calling homosexuals normal? I—

BARRY Ralph!

RALPH I'm in my house.... I'm at home, which is where you should be. I'm not far away. Come over if you want.... I have some cold cuts... beer.... Come over and we can talk some more . . . 'cause you and me, we're the same kind of people. I know you know what I'm talking about. . . . I have beer. Soup. I'm here. Come by later. I'll wait . . .

Barry stares at the mike. He starts to speak, but doesn't know what to say.

STU Barry, forty-five seconds left in the show! (*Barry is confused, still silent*) This is dead air, Barry, dead air . . .

Barry realizes that he wants "dead air." He stares at the mike, smiles to himself closes his eyes, waits. Long pause.

BARRY I guess we're stuck with each other. This is Barry Champlain. (*Signals to Stu. Theme music comes up. Barry gets up from his desk. Starts to leave, unsure of what he's just done. As he passes Stu's desk, he slaps his hand as he did when he arrived at the top of the show. In the doorway.*) Tomorrow, Stu . . .
STU Tomorrow, Bar . . .

Barry exits.

A quick news and weather report comes on. Stu packs it in. Susan Fleming's operator takes Stu's place and sets up. Dr. Susan Fleming enters, goes straight to the desk. Her show begins.

SUSAN This is Dr. Susan Fleming. . . . Before I take the first caller, I'd like to comment on something I saw on the way over to the station this evening. There was a man standing on a street corner, obviously mentally disturbed. . . . It made me think about something we don't often talk about . . .

Black out.

APPENDIX

Prerecorded Advertisements and Promos

Throughout *Talk Radio*, we played a number of prerecorded imitation "ads," news bits, logos, ID's. Here are some samples:

DIRTY HANDS (30 sec.)

(*Sound effects*)

I'm a man who works with his hands.... (*Clanging*) I work with steel and iron...gravel and grease.... Stuff that's tough on your hands, and lemme tell you, makes 'em real dirty....

At the end of the day, I need to get those hands clean... or the little lady won't let me in the house...

That's why I use... Uncle Roy's Special Soap... to get 'em clean and soft...

Uncle Roy's Special Soap...an old-fashioned formula for today's grease and grime...

NIGHTTALK Blurb

Coming up, in the next hour... Cleveland's most popular and controversial host of the airwaves: Barry Champlain...on Nighttalk!

WTLK Blurb 1

You're listening to Cleveland's Voice of the People: WTLK!

WTLK Blurb 2

When you've got something to say... or just want to listen... WTLK!

WTLK Blurb 3

This is WTLK... Cleveland's Voice of the People!

NIGHTTALK

(*Woman's voice*) The number for Nighttalk with Barry Champlain is 555-T-A-L-K.... Just let the phone ring, you'll be picked up when it's your turn to talk to Barry...

THE NEWS

This is Vince Farber with WTLK News Nightwatch... brought to you by Raddison's Muffler and Transmission shops.... In the headlines this evening, Croatian terrorists have hijacked another 747, this time an American Airlines jetliner headed for Quebec.... The Cleveland City Council voted unanimously today to reject the new toxic waste treatment bill that has been pending for five years.... An earthquake in Chile has killed seven hundred people.... Two deadly python snakes were released from the North Park Zoo last night.... A note was left behind claiming their release was prompted by cruelty to the animals.... And this just in.... Police raided a massive crack factory on the East Side.... Over sixty pounds of the drug were seized and thirty people arrested.... Finally, more on the North American Boy-Love Association that investigators believe has its headquarters in Shaker Heights.... Now there's some belief that the chapter was headed by a local Boy Scoutmaster! We'll be back with these and other breaking stories, after this:

RENDO (30 sec.)

RICH Hey, Bob, can I ask you something?
BOB Sure, Rich...

RICH How'd you ever quit smoking?

BOB I didn't.

RICH You didn't!

BOB Nope.

RICH Then how come your teeth are so white?

BOB Oh that! (*Laughs. Pause.*) I've got a good dentist.

ANNOUNCER Some people just can't tell the truth when it comes to clean teeth . . . and why should they? We'll let you in on a secret: it's not Bob's dentist that got his teeth so clean. . . . It was Rendo . . .

NEW ANNOUNCER Rendo . . . the tooth polish for smokers!

RICH So what's his number?

Bob's laughing to fade-out.

COLLAX AD (30 sec.)

Do you know what the number one ailment is that troubles men and women over forty all over America? No, it's not arthritis and not high blood pressure either. . . . It's chronic constipation . . . something most people don't want to talk about. . . . You probably don't either. That's why I'm here to tell you one word: *Collax*, the gentle laxative that works overnight to loosen up tense areas in your lower abdomen . . . naturally and without drugs. Collax uses a special patented ingredient—hydrogenated cellulose—that gets you moving fast . . . but not too fast! You don't need to talk about what worries you most when you know one word: *Collax*. *Collax*, your druggist has it, just ask him!

DORMEX AD (30 sec.)

As bedtime approaches, I have a rather appropriate question for you right now. . . . Do you have trouble falling asleep some nights?

Do you lie back worrying about everything, the world on your shoulders, your mind buzzing and unable to "turn off"? Do you find it difficult to clear your mind of the day's worries and get the rest and sleep you need to start the new day fresh?

Maybe you should try Dormex.

Dormex lets you empty your mind. Lets you find that special place where trouble is left far behind, cutting the chains of insomnia. Dormex contains no harmful ingredients, just three of nature's own soporifics: dilanium, perspex, and folic acid.

Try it, won't you? Available at all pharmacies and all Zeebo's department stores . . .

HARRY'S RESTAURANT (60 sec.)

Done as a "live spot," with Barry's voice prerecorded to sound live . . . very folksy.

Harry's Restaurant. For good warm food . . . served with a smile. Solid, nourishing, American-style cooking. Same cook for fifteen years, Joanie. . . . Joanie makes a leg of turkey with stuffing, gravy, and all the fixings that takes me right back to Mom's kitchen. And I'm sure that if you had a mom who used to make a lot of good-tasting things. . . . Well, why don't you go by and visit Harry's Restaurant because I bet you'll find a lot of that good stuff right there on the menu. It's really incomparable. Harry's. Now just for a second listen to what you get with their blue plate special: five ninety-five, you get your choice of soup—chicken noodle or soup du jour. Which you can trust will be excellent. You get bread, toast, or crackers. . . . They toast the bread, no extra charge. A salad. Dish of pickles. Bring a plate right to the table. Coleslaw, and of course you get the entree, your choice of chicken, meat loaf, or fresh fish. And with that you get your choice of french fries, baked or delmonico potatoes. Choice of two vegetables. Cup of coffee or tea or soft drink with your meal. And . . . dessert from the dessert bar. . . . Lots of good things to choose from. Can you beat it for five ninety-five? I don't think so. . . . Harry's Restaurant for good solid food. You'll be happy to leave a tip . . . for your waitress . . . at Harry's Restaurant, I know I always do. I go there as often as I can. . . . Really excellent. . . . Tell 'em Barry sent you.

DRINKING IN AMERICA

Drinking in America first appeared at the Institute of Contemporary Art in Boston (egged on by Bob Riley). From there it had a short stint at P.S. 122 in New York City (smiled at by Mark Russell), then went on a tour of Britain (with the help of Michael Morris of the London ICA) and finally came to roost at the American Place Theater in New York City, opening in January 1986, where I was directed by Wynn Handman.

JOURNAL

A man stands and reads out loud to the audience in a normal voice. Begin with improvised patter to the effect that this journal was found in an attic with some old college memorabilia.

April 11, 1971

Today I began to understand one of the immutable truths with regard to my own existence. Today I discovered that I am not a being surrounded by walls and barriers, but part of a continuum with all other things, those living and even those inanimate. I feel a new surge of desire for life, for living now, for getting out and becoming part of everything around me. I want to change the world and I know I can do it. I'm like a newborn baby taking his first steps. I was blind before to my inner self, my true desires, my own special powers and the universe itself. So many people live lives of pointless desperation, unable to appreciate that life is life to be lived for today, in every flower, in a cloud . . . in a smile.

I also realized today that Linda and I have to break up. I realize now that her lack of imagination has been holding me back. She's been trying to mold me into someone I will never be. She's too somber, too materialistic, too straight. She thinks that life must be lived in the straight and narrow, but she's wrong and I learned that today. Today I learned that life is an adventure for people with courage.

I guess I should back up for a minute here. I don't really know where to start. I guess everything began when I dropped that acid Mike gave me for my birthday. When I got off, I decided to take a bath, and I was watching the water, just thinking about how beautiful it looked, how I've never really noticed how beautiful bathwater looked before, when out of nowhere I heard this incredible music, like chimes.

Eventually I realized that it was the front doorbell and then I thought, I better go answer it, you never know. And I stood up and realized that I was wet and naked and then I thought, Hey, so what? What difference does it make, really, in the grand scheme of things? So I went to the door and it was this girl from down the street who I have never met before, and I forgot what she wanted, but I invited her in and—this is the really strange part—she came in.

So there we were in my parents' living room and I'm naked and she's beautiful so I made some tea. It took me around an hour to do it. Then we just sat and talked about everything and I realized that I have this incredible power over people. Almost messianic. She sat there and listened with these big beautiful brown eyes. And then I kissed her. And we were kissing and I was naked and I had this erection and she looked at it and suddenly she said she had to leave.

And I said, "Why?" And then we met each other's eyes for a long time and she said because she realized that I was a very special person and that she didn't want to ruin a special moment with something as common as sex. And I understood deep down what she meant. I understood that she meant that we were connecting in a much deeper way, that it was all too much for right now.

And she left, and I started to think . . . that I must be the kind of man that women find irresistible, that I am special, that I have powers others don't have, and that I can't let myself be hindered. I must connect with everything in this world that wants me. So, I just lay down on the floor, naked, tripping, and I could feel the power moving through me, as if the whole world lay under me just to hold me up. I was literally on top of the world. I felt like GOD.

That was around five hours ago and I'm pretty straight now. After I write this down, I'm going to call Linda and tell her it's over between us. Then I'm going to wait for my parents and tell them I'm dropping out of Boston University. There's really no point to a liberal arts degree now, with all the potential I have within me. I've decided to take my savings, a thousand dollars, and move to Portland, Oregon, for a while. I think that will be a good place to begin.

Until tomorrow . . .

SHANTI

AMERICAN DREAMER

A man stands in the middle of the stage. He knocks back an entire pint of wine in one swallow. He addresses passing cars.

Hey, bro! Hey, bro! bro! My MAN! How you doin' today? How you doin'?

I like dat car you're drivin', man . . . dat's a nice car. I like your car, man, I like your car. It's a nice car, man, how you doin' today? All right? ALL RIGHT!

I like your ol' lady sittin' dere too, man. HOW YOU DOIN', MAMA? Feelin' good? You're a beautiful lady, anybody ever tell you dat before? Bet he never tells you dat! *(pulls his crotch)*

How about you and me, we go aroun' da corner, drink a li'l bit more a dis T-Bird, I got a drop lef' here. How about it, whud-dyousay? You and me gonna party all night. Come on, baby! Come on!

Huh?

Say what? Hey, watch your mouth, sucker. You don't know who you talkin' to. You don't know who you talkin' to. . . . Come over here and say dat, bro, come on, right now, come over here! Hey. Hey. Hey. I was jus' sayin' dat shit to her, make her feel better, man . . . 'cause she's stuck wid YOU! . . .

Huh? Get outa da car. I don't have to take dat shit from you! Come on, get out. . . .

Gowan back to New Jersey, wherever you come from, man. Go fill some teeth, whatever you do. Get outa here. . . . You think you such a big deal . . . wid your rusty ol' Cadillac. Huh! And your flea-bitten ol' lady. Ugly ol' lady.

I DON'T NEED YOUR OL' LADY! What do I need her for?

Shit! Huh! Shit!

What do I need your ol' lady for? Got me plenty a ol' ladies!

Man, I got me so many ol' ladies . . . had to buy me a whole 'partment building jus' to fill it up wid my ladies, man! I got ladies in ev'ry 'partment. Fashion models. Blondes, brunettes, redheads. Look like dey jus' come outa *Vogue* magazine . . .

. . . all sittin' aroun' in deir 'partments, polishin' deir nails, sittin' waitin' aroun', waitin' aroun' fo' ME, man! Dey get up in da mornin', dey say to demselves, "Where is he? Where is my MAN! When's he gonna come see me? I need my KISS!" Dat's what dey say!

And I'm up on da top, in da penthouse, smokin' a cigarette, eatin' some Doritos, watchin' Donahue. . . . I need me a lady, I want me a *taste*, a little *squeeze*. Shit! I got me an intercom system. I press on my intercom system: "BUUUUUUP!—Yo! Renetta, get your butt up here, I wanna talk to you!"

See what I'm sayin? I got ladies all day long . . . all day long. . . .

Don't need your car neither. Got me plenty a cars. Got me . . . shit . . . got me a whole parkin' garage full a cars down da bottom a my buildin'.... Got me Mercedes, Lamborghinis, Maseratis, Volares... all dem kind a cars.... Don't even drive 'em. Jus' look at 'em.

I wanna drive aroun' I got me a limousine, bro. Stretch limousine. Long stretch limousine.... Long, long, loooonng stretch limousine. Ladies like 'em long. I got a long one, man.

Got me a chauffeur... he hates me, takes him all day to buff down one side a da limousine... all day he polishes one side... next day, he goes down de other side, dat's how long it is!

Got me a TV set in my limousine... 'frigerator, swimmin' pool, bar... fully stocked bar in my limousine... wid whiskey, good whiskey: Ol' Crow, Ol' Grandad... all da good kind, da old kind... COLT 45... ON TAP!... Perrier, dat Perrier shit.... Got it, don't drink it.

Got me toothpicks, napkins wid jokes on 'em, ice cubes... lil' plastic cups wid de chopped-up limes, chopped-up lemons, lil' red cherries... all dat shit. Got it. FRENCH WINE... from FRANCE!

(*He stumbles and falls to the floor.*)

I... I sit in da back a my limousine.... (*lies down*)... I lay down in da back a my limousine, I like dat even better.... I lay down... da ladies, dey all come down outa da building ... lie on me in da back a da limousine... lie down next to me, lie down on top a me... piled up, stacked up, squishin' me flat.... HUGE pile a ladies like a bowl a Jell-O!

We drive aroun'.... Got me a hookah... smoke my hookah: opium, hashish, cheebah, all dat shit packed in my hookah dere.... I smoke it up....

I get stoned... stoned... stoned outa my brain... and if I get too stoned out, I put my head back and da ladies dey sprinkle cocaine right down into my nostrils... jus' like dat! Right down dere. GOOD cocaine too. None a dat New Jersey dentist cocaine, man, I got da good kind... da kind da cops does, dat Miami cocaine... fill me right up, can't even breathe....

Den I put out my arm... dey gimme de French wine... intravenously... right down dere in my arm.... Open up da sky roof, watch da clouds... da birds flyin' aroun' up dere. We drive aroun'... turn on da TV set, see what's on *Wheel a Fortune* dere, see how Vanna be doin'... drive aroun' wid my ladies, I say... Ohhhhhhhhhhhhhhhhhhhh Yeah!

Dat's what I do! I don't NEED your ol' lady.... Got my own thing goin' here, I got da American Dream, see, I do what I wanna do, I do what EVERYBODY wants to do.... I drive aroun' all day long... in my limousine.... I get high... put my head back... watch da clouds... and I... pass out... I pass out. (*closes his eyes*)

WIRED

A sleepy man answers the phone in a nasal voice.

Yeah? Yeah. No, Arnie, you didn't wake me up. What time is it? Noon? *(looks at watch)* It's nine o'clock in the morning, Arnie, what are you calling me nine o'clock in the morning for? Yeah, yeah, it's noon where you are, it's nine o'clock in the morning here. Yeah, no . . . no, Arnie, you're in New York, I'm in Los Angeles. It's noon where you are, it's . . . no I'm not gonna explain it to you. I'm up, I'm up, Arnie, I'm up. . . . Listen, will you hold . . . Arnie, Arnie, wait a minute. . . . Arnie, Arnie, hold, Arnie, hold . . . hold on for a second, lemme get a cup of coffee here. . . . I'll be right—Arnie, hold on . . . lemme put you on hold. . . .

(He puts the phone down, groggily sets up lines of coke . . . cuts it.)

Arnie, you still there? Hold on. . . .

(snorts the coke)

Arnie? Lemme get the cream, hold on. . . .

(He pulls out a bottle of bourbon from a cabinet, pours a triple shot, drinks it. . . . He shakes out his arms, rolls his shoulders. . . . He wakes up, talking very fast. He pauses briefly, only to listen.)

Yeah Arnie, yeah, yeah, yeah. I'm here. I'm here. I'm here. I'm here, yeah, yeah, listen . . . listen . . . wait a minute, wait a minute . . . Arnie listen to me, will you listen to me? . . . You tell me how much money you got to spend, I'll tell you who you can get for your money....

...Who? Lee Marvin?! Lee Marvin?! You're not talking Lee Marvin money here, Arnie. You're not talking Lee Marvin money, you're talking Bullwinkle the Moose money to me here. For the amount you're talking about, maybe, just maybe, and I'm not making any promises here, I can get you, I don't know...Robert Vaughn...Vince Edwards...not Lee Marvin. Forget about Lee Marvin, gimme another name....

Who? Him? He's no good. he's a drug addict. He's a drug addict, Arnie...no, not that shit, the other thing....YES! Yes, yes, yes...the hard stuff, yes, with the needles and the spoons and the forks and the knives and the whole routine. Yes. Arnie, this guy's idea of a good time is throwing up. You understand what I'm telling you? You're gonna find him in a bathroom someplace turning blue. He's dead meat. Forget about him. You don't want him....

Huh? Of course it's a sad story, of course it's a sad story....What's the guy, twenty-six, twenty-seven years old, he makes a million dollars a picture, he's a drug addict....I should have his problems....I'm crying my eyes out. My tears are running onto the receiver here....FORGET ABOUT HIM! We'll go to his funeral....Gimme another name....

Who?...He's not available. He's got a broken hand....He broke it working out....He was working out on somebody's face, he broke his hand....The guy called him a homosexual. So what if he's a homosexual?...He's a homosexual who likes to go around punching people in the face and breaking his hand....Huh?...Yes, he's very macho....Yes, he's very virile. . . . Yeah, he's got a great moustache. . . . Listen, Arnie, the macho man has a broken hand, OK? He couldn't punch out Ricky Schroeder today. . . . He's not available. Gimme another name.

Who else?. . . He's dead. . . . He's dead. He's literally dead. . . . He fell off his boat in Malibu, a shark ate him. Of course it's ironic, of course it's ironic, Arnie, what are you telling me ironic? They had to cancel the whole series. . . . Arnie, I would love to do the deal with you, I'm sorry the fish ate the guy . . . go talk to the shark. . . . HE'S DIGESTED, HE'S NOT AVAILABLE!

Arnie, hold on, I got another call coming in . . . hold on. . . . (*He punches the hold button.*)

Yeah?. . . SID, SID, SID, SID, SID, SID! Listen to me: YES! Do you hear me saying yes? I said yes. Yes. You have Richard Chamberlain. . . . Richard Chamberlain, The *Bhopal Story*, it's gonna happen. . . . Yes, *The Bhopal Story: The Tragic Story of a Misunderstood Multinational* starring Richard Chamberlain, name over the title, one hundred percent of the title, filmed on location in India with a cast of a thousand beggars. You're gonna make a million bucks on this thing, Sid. . . . Yes, you have the blind beggars . . . yes, you got the crippled beggars. . . . Will you get off my case, it's gonna be the greatest miniseries in the history of miniseries.

Huh? What do you mean you have some more people you want me to look at? Who?. . . Who's he?. . . The greatest actor in India? I never heard of him. . . . I never heard of him, Sid, I don't care if he's Mahatma Gandhi's grandson, if I never heard of him he's not coming in on this picture. . . . Because he's an unknown, that's why.... Why is he unknown? Because he doesn't have a name.... Sid, we're talkin' Richard Chamberlain here, OK? One of the greatest, if not the greatest, American actors of our time! I cannot have this great actor acting opposite some two-bit, unknown Hindu! I don't care if everyone in India has his face tattooed on their chests, he's an unknown in the States.... Wait a minute, wait a minute.... Sid, Sid, Sid, Sid, Sid ... can I ... can I ... can I get a word in edgewise here for a second?

This guy, is he in the union? Is he in SAG? All right, listen, bring him down to the set, we'll give him some water to carry around, he can do a little Gunga Din routine for us there.... It's the best I can do, Sid.... Sid, I'm getting off the phone.... Have a nice time in India, watch out for the prime rib.... OK, yeah, ha ha.... *(punches the hold button again)*

Yeah, Arnie, I'm still here....

Who? No I won't talk to him for you. Because he's insane, that's why.... Why is he insane? He's insane because he thinks he's God.... Have you talked to God lately, Arnie? Let me tell you something about "God." ... He's an egomaniac.... And after a couple of drinks, he's a shitty actor too....

Arnie, the man sits there on the set like Buddha ... telling everybody what to do! He's telling the actors what to do, he's telling the director what to do, he's telling the lighting man what to do.... He's got an answer for everybody.... He's got the answer for everybody's problems.... you know what his answer to everybody's problems is? ... HIS SCHLONG, that's what it is!

Fucking the girls?...He's fucking the girls, he's fucking the boys, he's fucking the stuntmen, you bend over in front of him, he'll be fucking you too, Arnie!...

Listen, Arnie, the guy is a promiscuous egomaniac, he should be locked up in a padded cell....I DON'T CARE HOW TALENTED HE IS! I DON'T CARE!...BECAUSE I HAVE MY PRINCIPLES. (*He drops to his knees and pounds the floor.*) Listen, Arnie, I'm gonna burst a blood vessel here in another second....Just forget about him....

Look, I can get you Lee...as a favor, he'll do it as a favor for me...uh, hundred thou....Hundred thou—but only for five minutes. Arnie, I'm talkin' Lee Marvin here, one of the greatest if not the greatest American actor...that's it....I don't want to talk about it, Arnie, if you're not gonna be rational...no... no...I'm getting off....NO! I'm getting off, Arnie, hundred thou and that's 'cause you're my friend....I love you too, Arnie, and from me that's a compliment....Yeah....Arnie, Arnie, Arnie....Bye.

(*hangs up*)

CERAMIC TILE

A man is standing, arms outstretched, holding a champagne bottle. He's talking in a Texas accent to someone, a girl.

Whoooeeee! I'm feelin' good tonight, I'm feelin' fine tonight. Come here, come here, come here, come darling...come on, come on, give Daddy, give Daddy a kiss...give me a kiss....Come on. Come on. Come on....Do ya love me? Do ya love me? Do ya love me? Sure ya do....Come on, have some more champagne, here, darlin'. You gotta have yourself some more champagne! Come on....

(He gives a big whoozy kiss, and rocks on his heels.)

YEAH? WHO IS IT? COME ON IN, DOOR'S UNLOCKED!... Yeah...just a, just, OK, just put it, bring it on into the room there, that's OK. Just put it over by the bed there, that'll be fine. Yeah. OK. Ummmm. Looks delicious. Yessir. Heh heh. All right. OK. Yeah....Look, buddy, I'll sign for it later, give yourself five bucks, OK? Thank you too. All right. OK. All right. I will. OK. Heh heh....Oysters do do that....Yeah. Thanks a lot. Good night, buddy. Yeah, all right, I'm a little busy now so...all right....OK....Lock the door on your way out....Thank you too. OK. All right. LOCK THE DOOR!

Where were we? Oh yeah, you gotta have some more of this good champagne here darling. You don't have some more champagne, I'm gonna have to drink it all myself! I drink it all myself, I'm gonna throw up all over your pretty party dress there. WHOOOOOEEEEEE! I'm feeling good tonight! I'm feelin' fine tonight.

(coughs, slumps in a chair)

Michelle. Michelle? . . . Michelle! See, I told you I'd remember your name!

Turn around for me a second, Michelle, lemme take a look at you. . . . Lemme take a look at you, go ahead, turn around. Yeah. . . . You're one hell of a good-looking girl, aren't you darlin'? You're just about the most beautiful girl I seen . . . the last twenty-four hours. You know that? You are.

You got beautiful breasts. You got a beautiful behind. You got everything right where it belongs and plenty of it, don't you, huh? (drinks) You can stop turning around now, Michelle.

How old you say you were?

Just a babe outa the woods, eh?

Guess. . . . Go ahead, guess. . . .

Forty-seven years old. My wife says I look like I'm sixty. She says being on the road all the time makes you get older faster. She thinks I enjoy being on the road. I hate being on the road. . . .

Tell you a secret. Tomorrow's my daughter's fourteenth birthday . . . and I can't be there. Can't be there at my own little girl's birthday party 'cause I gotta be here at this convention.

You know why I gotta be at this convention, Michelle? Because I am an industrial ceramic tile salesman. . . . And when you're an industrial ceramic tile salesman you gotta do one thing and you gotta do it real well. You gotta sell industrial ceramic tile. That's what I do, see, I sell tile. . . . I sell tile all the way from Tampa to San Diego. I sell tile and I sell a lot of it. I go to every little sales meeting, every convention, I go out there and bust my ass. . . .

It's a dog-eat-dog world out there, Michelle, and I go out there and I bite. . . . I bite as hard as I can and I don't let go 'til I make a sale. 'Cause I'm good. 'Cause I'm the best.

I work hard, Michelle. I work hard, you work hard. Everybody in the world works hard. Everybody in the whole world works hard . . . except my wife. My wife, my wife thinks money grows in checkbooks . . . she thinks her job is spending the money I earn. She thinks it's easy for me to go out there on the road, kill myself to bring back a couple of bucks so she can sit by the poolside flipping through her Saks Fifth Avenue catalogue picking out sterling-silver eggcups and fur-lined Cuisinarts. . . . She just sits there all day trying to figure out where to waste my money next. She thinks that's her job and . . .

What am I talking about her for when I'm here with you, right?

What do you do when you're not doing this, Michelle? Uh-huh. Good. You keep going to school. It's important to go to school. No future in this escort business, I'll tell you that. You keep going to school, Michelle, because . . . I want you to. You're a beautiful, sensitive girl and I wanna see good things happen to you, so you keep going to . . .

WHAT'S THAT LOOK? What's that look? I know, I know, I know what you're thinking....I know what you're thinking....You think I'm bullshitting you, don't you? You're looking at me you're thinking: here's another middle-aged, overweight, half-drunk...ceramic tile salesman....I know, I know....Well, let me tell you something, little girl, I may be middle-aged and I may be a little round at the edges and I may be feeling pretty good tonight...but I'm very different than the rest of these idiots you see here at this convention... don't confuse me with these salesmen guys.

I'm nothing like them, and I'll tell you why....Because... see...I...you're looking at...you're in the same room with...the NUMBER ONE ceramic tile salesman in the United States of America. Numero uno. I sell more tile than all these guys put together. I sell more tile than anybody in the whole United States of America....I probably sell more tile than anybody in the whole world!

Now think about that...that's a lot of tile. And I sell it all. Because I'm good, I'm the best, I'm special. And the reason why I'm special is...'cause I care about people. I do. And I care about you, Michelle. Because you're special too....

You know, tonight, when I came into the hotel, I thought to myself, I'm just gonna have a couple of drinks, go up to my room, pass out. But I saw you standing down there in the lobby, and I said to myself, "There is a beautiful, sensitive, intelligent, sophisticated girl...a beautiful girl with beautiful blue eyes...green eyes, beautiful green eyes...there's a girl I could talk to tonight." That's what I said to myself. There's a girl I can talk to.

Because I'll be honest with you, Michelle, I just need a little companionship. I'm just a lonely guy...just a lonely little cowboy....

You know, every morning I wake up, I'm in a different hotel room...the first thing I hear is the alarm clock ringing by the bed, the first thing I see...the toilet...then I see the cable TV set down by the end of the bed...luggage on the floor, maid knockin' on the door, I got a headache and a hangover and I don't know where the hell I am!

Now if I don't know where I am, how the hell's anybody else supposed to know where I am? I feel like I'm the last man left in the whole world...and I get lonely, Michelle....I get real lonely....

Come here, come here, come here, baby, don't stand there all night, come here and give Daddy a hug. Come on.

Oh yeah...ummmm that's nice....

SHIT! I'm jus' about gonna pass out on you here, Michelle! (*He slumps in his chair.*)

Lissen, Michelle, it was great talkin' to you, I want to tell you you're one hell of a stimulating conversationalist, you know...and I'll let you get out of here now...and I just want to tell you it was great...and uh...Michelle, before you go, though, uh...jus' so that hundred bucks don't go to a total waste, do you think you could do a little something for me right now...jus' so, jus' so your boss knows you're working? (*wink*) Huh? She tell you what I like, right? Think you could do a little bit of that for me right now? Huh? Just a quick one? Just a nice slow quick one?

Yeah, you got the idea . . . oh! Ummmmmmm. That's it. Yes. Oh, I feel better already. . . . Oh . . . I'll tell you something, Michelle . . . nothing worse . . . than being . . . lonely. . . .

COMMERCIAL

A man stands before a microphone. He holds a piece of paper in his hand. A voice speaks to him from a raspy loudspeaker.

VOICE: (click) What do you think, Eric? (click)

ERIC: Looks good. . . .

VOICE: (click) Yeah, uh . . . you wanna try it for me one time here, just throw something off? (click)

ERIC: We laid down more than one before. Which one did you like?

VOICE: (click) I'm sorry, what was that? (click)

ERIC: We did more than one take, which one did you like?

VOICE: (click) Uh . . . I think we liked the third one. (click)

ERIC: Warm?

VOICE: (click) Macho. But with a smile. You're selling virility. (click)

ERIC: Gotcha. I think I can do that.

VOICE: (click) Good . . . uh, you wanna give Jimmy a level? (click)

ERIC: Sure. (reading) Krönenbräu. Krönenbräu. Krönenbräu. Krönenbräu. Krönenbräu. Krönen—

VOICE: (cutting in): (click) That's fine. OK. So, uh, let's try it once, OK? (click)

ERIC: I'm ready.

VOICE: (click) Remember, Eric, this is the voice inside your head. The guy wants to get laid and you've got the secret. (click)

ERIC: Wants-to-be-part-of-the-crowd kind of guy.

VOICE: (click) Right. OK? Jimmy will give you the cue. No slate. (click)

ERIC: You've worked hard to get . . . I'm sorry, can we start over again? I'm not . . . concentrating. . . .

VOICE: (click) OK. We're still running. (click)

ERIC: You've worked hard to get where you are today and you've still got a long way to go before you get to the top. . . . You want your life to be *good* . . . so you surround yourself with the best . . . the very best . . . in clothes, in food, in people. . . . You know you're going to get there someday . . . and when you do, you'll say "good-bye" to your companions of a less prosperous time. But there is one thing you will never leave behind. . . .

And that's your beer: Krönenbräu . . . always superb, always fulfilling, always the best . . . because you're the best. . . .

Just taste it and feel its *strength* fill you. . . .

Ahhhh. . . . Krönenbräu. The thing you have before everything else. Krönenbräu. The beer of kings.

VOICE: (click) OK, Eric, sounds good. Nice and warm, but macho, I'll buy it. . . . Just gimme the tag three times, OK? and then we'll uh . . . play it back. I think we'll be all done for the day. . . . I think that's all right. . . . We're gonna, we're gonna keep it. . . . (click)

ERIC: That's it? Great. OK, tag three times:

(clears throat)

(normal voice) Ahhhhhh. . . . Krönenbräu. The thing you have before everything else. Krönenbräu. The beer of kings.

(peppy voice) Ahhhhhh. . . . Krönenbräu. The thing you have before everything else. Krönenbräu. The beer of kings.

(deep voice) Ahhhhh. . . . Krönenbräu. The thing you have before everything else. Krönenbräu. The beer of kings.

(looks up for approval, fade out)

MELTING POT

A man in a V-neck T-shirt stands and gesticulates with his arms, shouting with a Greek accent.

LISA! LISA! Get this guy over here.... What do you want? What do you want? Huh? Cup of coffee? What else? That's it, cup of coffee?... LISA, get this bum cup of coffee....

Where the hell is Jesus?* *(shouts at the floor)* JESUS! JESUS! What are you doing down there?... Shooting up? Jerking off? Come on, come out of there.... What rat?... Leave the rat, if it's dead leave it.... Come up here now, come on, come here, I want to show you something.

OK, come here.... What is this? Huh? What is this mess? French fries in the fat, french fries on the floor, french fries in the sink, everyplace french fries. Mess, mess, mess, mess, mess, mess. Eh? Huh? Look at me when I'm talking to you! Look at me. Don't look at girl over there, look at me....

Who teach you to make mess like this? I don't teach you to make mess. You want Health Department come in here, they close us up, they say, "George too dirty, close up!"?

I show you how to make french fries, you don't make no more mess, all right....

Yeah, yeah, yeah, yeah, yeah.... I know you know, I know you know, you know everything, you genius!... George show

*Pronounced Hey-soose.

you how to make french fries, no more mistake, all right? No more messy. Yeah, yeah, you watch me, mister. . . .

Take bag, all right, cut corner on bag, all right? Yeah, I know you know, smart guy. . . . Einstein, you watch me. Take bag, put in basket, all right? (*His arms flail wildly.*)

In . . . in . . . not all over . . . in the basket. One shake. Put back, take basket, put in fat, all right? Cooking. . . . Cooking. . . . Cooking. . . . Easy, nothing to it! . . . Cooking. . . . Cooking. . . .

Then shake, shake, bim, bim, boom, boom, zip, zip! Back in. Cooking. . . . Cooking. . . . Cooking. . . . All right, take it out . . . brown, white, don't make no difference, nobody eat it anyway. . . .

All right, now you show me. Show me, I want to see, come on. I don't got all day here, please, I'm busy. . . .

(*watching*) All right, OK, yaaaaa, ummmmm, all right, put it in, ummmmm, yaaaaaa, OK.

You know, I don't have to hire you, you know. Lisa, she tell me you good.

That Chinese guy, he was great! Buck an hour that guy, huh? . . . Too bad he die on me. . . .

Come on, come on, put it back now, you're spilling, you're spilling! . . .

You know what your problem is, Jesus? You Puerto Rican. You go back whenever you want to go back. You come, you go, you don't need green card, you be citizen when you want be citizen. I can't go back. I have to stay in America. You want to stay in America, you have to work all the time. . . .

I want to be big success in America. I work sometimes twenty-four hours a day, I work. Sometimes I don't eat, I don't sleep, I don't piss. Nothing. Working all the time. That's it. You know what I'm saying?

You don't work all the time, you know what's gonna happen to you? You gonna be like all these these these bums, these junkies, these winos . . . they come in here, they hang around all the time, night and day. "Gimme cup a coffee. Gimme cup a coffee. Gimme glass a water—I wanna shoot up. I wanna throw up! Cup a coffee. Glass a water. Cup a coffee. Glass a water. . . ."

You want cup a coffee? You want glass a water? You go back to Puerto Rico. They got water there, they got coffee, all day long. You want to be in America, you work. That's it. Working all the time. All right? That's it. Work.

No time for this . . . wine . . . this drugs . . . this hanging around, pinball, disco, girlfriends, TV, movies . . . bullshit.

(pounds chest) WORK! WORK! WORK! WORK! WORK!

You work, you make money, you buy house . . . you go in melting pot, you melt. That's the American way. You know what I'm saying? Think about these things. All right. All right.

Come on, OK, that's good. A little burn, but OK. All right, that be your lunch today. . . . Double order french fries. Is good for you. Lots of vitamins. . . . (*pats Jesus on the back*)

Don't worry. Don't worry. Don't cry. You learn how to make french fries, don't worry . . . two, three years you make as good as George. Good boy.

LISA! LISA! Take over for me, I'm going to the bank, I gotta make deposit. . . .

(*walks off*)

OUR GANG

A tough guy, holding a beer bottle, T-shirt sleeves rolled up, struts onstage.

(turning) Tony, you goin' to the store? Get me a pack a cigarettes, will ya? Marlboro . . . hard pack. And get me a Ring-Ding
too, I'm hungry. . . . Get me a Diet Pepsi too, I'm starved, didn'
have no breakfast or nothin'. . . . Please? Please? Come on man,
I got a hangover man, I'm disabled. I'll pay ya back later. . . .
Yer a saint man. . . .

(turning and sipping his beer) I'm all right. . . . I'm all right. . . .
Where were you last night, Joe? We was lookin' all over the
place for you. It was FUCKIN' GREAT man! You missed the
whole fuckin' thing. Me and Frankie and Sally and Joanie, we
had these 'ludes, Frankie got 'em outa the drugstore where he
works. . . . So we took these 'ludes, I figure let's take the 'ludes,
take my car, drive up the highway, smoke a couple a "j's,"
drink a couple a beers, listen to some Bruce on the radio, you
know, make a quiet night of it, stay outa trouble, right? Right.

So we're drivin' around, I'm not gettin' off on the 'ludes, right?
So I turns to Frankie, I says, "Frankie, I'm not gettin' off on
these 'ludes." Frankie turns to me, he says, "Don't worry man,
you will. . . . " You know with that, like, wisdom that Frankie's
got, he just knows stuff. . . .

So I'm drivin', I'm drivin', waitin' for the 'ludes to kick in and
I looks down and I see I got this little piece a dirt on my shoe.
And you know me, I'm neat and clean, I don't like gettin'
nothin' on my clothes or nothin'. So I'm drivin', I keep lookin'

down at this piece a dirt . . . piece a dirt's drivin' me crazy. It's like me and this piece a dirt we got this thing goin' on here between us. . . . I'm lookin' down I keep seein' this piece a dirt. It's lookin' at me, I'm lookin' at it. Back and forth, drivin' me nuts. I'm mesmerized by the dirt. So, I start scratchin' the dirt off my shoe. . . . I'm scratchin', I'm scratchin'. . . . Got my hand on the wheel, drivin' the car, not fuckin' aroun' or nothin'.

Scratchin', scratchin' . . . all of a sudden. . . . out a fuckin' no-place: BANG! This guardrail comes up the front a the car! Car starts spinnin' aroun', chicks is screamin' in the backseat, cars honkin' their horns all around me and shit. . . . BOOM! We go over the guardrail, we're on the other side of the highway now, goin' down the highway . . . cars blinkin' their headlights at me and shit . . . you know, like I don't know I'm on the wrong side of the road!? People are so stupid! BANG! We go down the side of the road, into this you know, valley-gully thing, down by the side of the road. ZING! Car comes to a stop.

I gets outa the car. Frankie gets outa the car. Sally gets outa the car. Joanie gets outa . . . everybody gets outa the car. Everybody's cool, everybody's fine, everybody's healthy, right? Great. . . . The car, Joe. You had to see the car, man. Everything was gone from the outside of the car, you know? The bumpers was gone, and the headlights was gone, and the handles was gone and the license plate . . . the car was one big scrape. It looked like, it looked like . . . you know E.T.? Little fuckin' E.T.? It looked like fuckin' E.T.'s head. (laughs)

Frankie comes . . . Frankie comes over to the car, he comes over. He looks at the car like this, he says, "Fuck the fuckin' car, man, the fuckin' car's fucked!" Right? (laughs) With that razor wit of his, you know, *zing!* The guy's a fuckin' word-master . . . thinkin' all the time. . . .

All right, so I figure, let's ditch the car, we're holdin' 'ludes, let's get outa here before the cops show . . . so we start hitchin' down the highway. . . .

Nobody's pickin' us up. . . . I don't know why. . . . Joanie's just got a little blood runnin' down her face, that's it. Nothin'. So we're standin' there, finally, this van shows up. Big peace sign painted on the side, flowers painted . . . yeah, yeah, that's it, a hippie van, like outa prehistoric times. . . . Door pops open, guy drivin' the van, Joe, you had ta see this guy. He's got hair down to his butt, he's got a headband on, incense, flowers, beads, Grateful Dead music on the tape player, you know, complete asshole. . . .

We figure, what the hell, why not? So we all jumps inside this guy's van. Joanie gets in the front seat, the rest of us gets in the backseat. We start drivin'.

Joe. The guy starts rollin' these joints. You had to see these joints, they were huge, the size of ya dick. No, even bigger, the size of MY dick, enormous! (*laughs*) Monster joints, made outa some kind of weed, I never smoked weed like this before in my life. The strongest weed I ever smoked. Like from one of those weird oriental places, like Taiwan. . . . Taiwan weed, that's what it was. Taiwan weed, all right. . . . Smoke one toke a this shit, ya blind for the rest of ya life! Good weed, strong weed.

Me and Frankie, we each roll up a monster joint of this stuff and we're in the backseat, blowin' smoke rings around each other's head. Like getting completely wasted, just wasted outa our brains, vaporized. Meltin'-into-the-upholstery kind of thing...oxygen-tent time, you know? We're doin' experiments on our brain cells...like how many can you kill in one toke? (*laughs*)

Totally, totally screwed into the fuckin' ground, blown inside out, comatose, right? Even the Grateful Dead music's startin' ta sound good.... "Truckin' with da Doo-Dah Man!" (*laughs, then starts coughing*) Blasted! Then...then the 'ludes kick in!

All right. Now, check this out. Party time, right? OK. So we're drivin' along, havin' this good time, and all of a sudden this guy, this hippie guy, he reaches over, he puts his hand on Joanie's leg! Frankie's sittin' in the backseat, he goes like, "Hey, man, take ya hand off my girlfriend's leg!" Right?

The guy turns around to Frankie, he says: "Hey, man...(*shoots his middle finger*)...fuck you!" Right? To Frankie he says this....

So what's Frankie gonna do? He takes his knife out, he opens it up, he goes: "No, man, fuck you!" Right?

The guy reaches into the glove compartment, pulls out a handgun, points it at Frankie's head, he says: "No, man, FUCK YOU!"

I'm fuckin' shittin' my pants, right, 'cause you do not fuckin' fuck with Frankie!...You know what I'm talkin' about? We're in a movin' vehicle here, we've got a loaded gun here, I'm not feelin' good about this....

Frankie's sittin' there like a stick a dynamite, just vibratin', right? The guy turns around ta look at the road for one second,

Frankie takes the knife, bing! Cuts the guy behind the ear.... Little tiny cut, nothin' cut, hardly bleedin'.

Guy gets pissed off. Pulls the van to the side of the road. Says, "Everybody outa the van right now!" The van's stopped by the side of the road. He's wavin' the gun around in front a Frankie's face....

What's Frankie gonna do? He takes his knife, closes it up nice.... (punches) BANG BANG! BANG! BANG! BANG! BANG! BANG! The guy's head.... (kicks) BOOM! BOOM! BOOM! BOOM! BOOM! BOOM! Kicks the guy outa the van. WHAM! WHAM! WHAM! WHAM! WHAM! WHAM! In the ribs, guy's on the ground. Frankie just bends over, picks up the gun, gets back in the van, we're outa there. FRANKIE!!! (laughing)

We leave the guy in the middle of the highway lookin' like the Woodstock revolution or somethin'. "GET A HAIRCUT, HIP-PIE !" (laughing)

So now we got the guy's van.... So Frankie's drivin', he takes the van down off the highway, so no cops, right? There's a little road down into these woods. Frankie's drivin'... real careful: "Oh, there's a tree!" BANG! "Oh, there's another tree!" CRASH! "There's a rock!" BOOM! Beatin' the hell outa this guy's van.... CRACK! We break the axle....

We're in the middle of the woods, we don't know where we are.... Frankie gets outa the van, he looks at the axle, he goes: "Don't worry, man, I can fix it!"

He gets in the back of the van, he looks around, finds a can of gasoline and starts splashin' the gasoline all over the inside of the van. . . . He turns to me, he says, "Richie, can I see ya cigarette fa a second?" I couldn't figure out what he wants my cigarette for. . . . He takes one puff outa my cigarette, flips it in the van. . . .

BOOM! The van blows up! Joe, you had to see this thing, man, it was nice, man. It was really nice. . . . Fireball, ten, fifteen feet high . . . like this . . . colors in it and everything. It was beautiful, one of the most beautiful things I ever seen. . . .

Plus we's in the woods, right? You ever been in the woods before, real woods? Nice in the woods. . . . Not like Central Park. . . .

This fireball's burnin' like this in the middle of the woods, and we're in this clearin' and all around us you got like . . . trees, you know, with leaves on 'em and stuff, and like the flames, they're like reflectin' up on the leaves, you know. Then up over ya head, ya got like stars . . . and it's quiet, ya know, real quiet in the woods. You don't hear nothin' . . . just, like, maybe a headlight poppin' or the windshield wipers meltin' onto the hood . . . nice, you know, quiet. . . .

And I'm just standin' there, the fire's burnin', the stars, the 'ludes, my friends standin' next ta me . . . it was like spiritual or somethin'. I never felt so calm in my life. . . .

Joanie was lookin' in the flames, she said she could see Jim Morrison's face like floatin' in there.

Frankie's totally into it. Frankie's spiritual, you know. Ever talk to Frankie about Satan? He knows all about Satan.

He turns to me, he goes like this, he goes, "Here man, take this."

I says, "Frankie, I can't take any more shit, I'm gonna fall down!"

He says, "Take it, man, take it. Trust me, it'll wake you up. . . ."

So I takes the stuff, I figures it's crystal or speed or pep pills, somethin' harmless like that . . . it's triple-strength LSD! Acid, we're doin' acid. I haven't done acid for at least three . . . weeks. . . .

ZOOOOOOM! Everything's meltin' and weird and stuff. . . . Plus it's the woods, so you got trees and rocks and crazy shit like that, right? Not like in the city where everything's nice, easy to figure out. . . . You're walkin' along, smashed outa ya brains . . . a little squirrel runs out . . . looks like a fuckin' rhinoceros! (He jumps.)

And Frankie, he's still got the guy's gun, right? So he's walkin' along. . . . BANG, BANG, BANG, BANG, BANG! Shootin' in the air, trying to see how far up the bullet goes. . . .

Anyways, to make a long story short, we ends up comin' to this big field. . . . Beautiful field with like a beautiful farmhouse in the middle of it, the kind of farmhouse, like, the Pepperidge Farm guy, he'd live in that farmhouse, right? Nice farmhouse. . . .

Frankie says: "Check this out. He goes up to the farmhouse . . . (laughing) . . . he's such a practical joker . . . goes right up to the front door . . . doo-doo-doo-doo-doo . . . rings the door-bell and this little old lady comes to the front door. And like, Frankie, he takes the gun, he goes . . . he goes like this: "Helter skelter, run fa shelter, let us in!"

(laughing) We go waltzing into these people's house, we're like completely bonked outa our brains, we don't know where we are or nothin'.

This old guy's like comin' down the stairs puttin' on his bath-robe, doin' this like, you know, "What's goin' on down here?" kind of thing, right? "Can I help you boys?" He's tryin' to threaten us or somethin', right?

Frankie takes the gun, he wasn't gonna hurt the guy or nothin', he just takes the gun goofin' aroun', takes the gun and goes up to the old guy like this, he goes (pointing his finger): "Say one more word, Grampa, I'll blow ya brains all over the wall-paper!" (laughing) "Blow ya brains all over the wallpaper"? Where does Frankie think this shit up? He's so funny!

Anyways, we gets the guy and the old lady, we put 'em on the floor, we cut their phone wires, tie 'em up with the phone wire, like on Kojak. Frankie's still into it. He's standin' over them with the gun: "We're the Charles Manson gang. If you tell anybody about us, we're gonna come back and burn ya house down!" I'm like, "Come on, Frankie, time to get outa here, man. You don't want to give these people the wrong im-pression about us or nothin'. Enough's enough!"

So anyway, we take their car keys, we take some booze, we hightail it outa there over ta Frankie's father's house. It's like four o'clock in the morning or somethin'. . . .

Huh?

Nah, his dad ain't home at four in the morning! His dad's an alcoholic, man, he's on the street all night drinking his face off. You ever meet his dad? . . . Aw, yeah, it's pathetic, he's got like a beer in one hand and a whiskey in the other. Yeah, I feel bad for Frankie, his father's so fucked up.

Anyway, so we like got the stereo on full-blast, we're dancin', we're partyin', me and Frankie and everybody, we're havin' a great time. . . . Joanie's in the bathroom throwin' up, 'cause she's got lousy tolerance. Couple a 'ludes, acid, it goes to her head.

OK. Now Sally starts comin' on to me, right? I been tryin' to make this chick for three months or somethin' and now she's standin' in front a me doin' this like, "Richie, Richie, I really want to go home with you, I need you, I want you. I love you. Take me home right now . . . uh-uh-uh-uh-uh!" Like this, right?

I'm standin' there, I'm lookin' at her thinkin' to myself: She's beautiful . . . she's stoned . . . she don't know what she's sayin' . . . her eyes aren't even open, fah cryin' out loud. (*pause*) What the hell, go for it!"

So I take the car keys, I start drivin' her home. . . . She's hot! She's got her hands down my pants, she's got her tongue in my ear, she's drivin' me crazy. . . .

I'm drivin' as fast as I can . . . six, seven miles an hour at least. (*laughs*)

I finally get to in front of her parents' house and when I turns to her to like start romanticizing her and shit, you know, I turns and . . . she's passed out! She's on the floor, curled up in a ball under the glove compartment, she's under there. . . .

So what am I gonna do? I'm a gentleman, I don't mess with unconscious broads. . . . So I gets outa the car, I go around, I pulls her outa the car. . . .

I brings her up to the front door of her parents' house and her parents they got like a regular front door and they got a screen door, you know? So I opens up the screen door, and I like wedge her up between the two doors . . . lock the door, ring the doorbell . . . get the hell outa there!

(laughs, slaps hands with Joe)

(unzips his fly, turns his back to the audience, looks down)

So anyways, listen, Joe, we're goin' out again tonight man, you should come along with us. . . . It's a lot of fun. . . . You know, it'd be a good time, Frankie likes you and everything. . . . (zipping up) Oh, yeah, Frankie wanted me to ask you one thing . . . uh (adjusts his cock in his pantleg) . . . you got a car?

NO PROBLEMS

A man comes out to center stage and in a normal voice casually addresses the audience.

I have no problems. I'm happy with life. Things are fine as far as I'm concerned. I know some people have problems, some people have quite a few. I, fortunately, have none.

First of all, I'm in perfect health. I just got back from the doctor's office, he gave me a completely clean bill of health. He checked me from top to bottom. He couldn't believe what great shape I'm in. I guess all that jogging and bran paid off. He even checked my teeth...no cavities...so I'm in perfect health.

I have a good job. It's a, uh...I guess you would call it a "semicreative" job, very little pressure to perform. I put in about forty hours a week...when I want to. I have the weekends off every week, three weeks' paid vacation in the summer. I get paid very well for what I do. It's a good job. I like it.

My wife and I have been married fifteen years. We're very loving and have a very supportive relationship. My wife's a very attractive, a very lovely lady. We have a great sex life, if you have to know. I don't fool around. Wasn't it Paul Newman who said, "Why go out for hamburger when you can have steak at home?" I subscribe to that theory.

Our daughter's eleven and she's doing very well in school. She gets very high grades, has a lot of friends. Besides her school work she also uh . . . she's also studying modern dance, violin. Next month she starts her Latin lessons. She's a very precocious, very pretty little girl. We like her very much.

Our parents are alive on both sides and uh . . . we all like each other. None of this "mother-in-law" stuff in our household. We all enjoy each other's company. They're all retired now. They worked hard and saved during their active years and now they're enjoying a . . . "golden harvest" so to speak. Certainly no burden on us, we're very proud of them.

Our friends are all happy and healthy as far as we know. We usually see them around once a week. We go over to their house and uh . . . have dinner over at their house. Or at our house. I like to cook. I'm kind of a gourmet chef. I like to cook things like uh . . . I don't know . . . uh, tortellini with sun-dried tomatoes or uh . . . arugula salad with endives, something you wouldn't think of . . . that's my cooking style. Or we go out and see a movie . . . something with Meryl Streep in it or . . . uh, a play, a Sam Shepard play usually or one of those one-person shows or magic or juggling plays. We like them, there's so many to choose from. . . . Or we go bowling. We all like to bowl. They're very nice people, we've had a lot of good times with them.

So that's it, uh . . . our neighborhood is safe and clean. We have an excellent town council, an activist school committee (and that's important!). Ummm . . . fire department, police department, garbage disposal . . . all top-rated.

The house is in good shape, just had a new boiler put in last year, there's nothing wrong with the house. The Volvo's running smoothly, nothing wrong with the car. So uh. . . .

I mean, there are times when, uh, I mean, I'll be honest...
there are times when I am concerned about all the, uh, you
know, all the trouble there is in the world these days. You
know, you turn on the news and uh...it's disturbing, you
know...and nobody likes being disturbed. I make myself
watch it because I know I should. For their sake.

And I worry about it all. But then I just think to myself, There's
always been trouble, we didn't invent it, you know, and uh, I
should just be thankful for all the good things I have in my life.
Those people are doing their thing out there, whatever it is
and uh, well anyway, I...I guess this isn't really the point....

The future looks good. We're going to have the house paid off
in ten years. We're buying a little condo down by the water,
kind of as an investment/vacation/retirement thing. We're really excited about that....

Ummmm, we've got money in a pension fund, so we're cool
there...insurance...some stock.

Like I said, I have no problems. None. I'm happy. I'm healthy.
I love my wife, I love my kid...good job...no problems.

That's what it's all about...I guess.

GODHEAD

A strip of white light falls across a man seated in pitch-black, holding a micro-phone. He speaks slowly in a guttural voice.

The way I see it, it's a fucked-up world, it's not going anyplace, nothing good is happening to nobody, you think about it these days and nothing good is happening to anybody and if something good is happening to anybody, it's not happening to me, it's not happening to myself.

The way I see it, there be this man, some man sitting in a chair behind a desk in a room somewhere down in Washington, D.C. See, and this man, he be sitting there, he be thinking about what we should do about crime rate, air pollution, space race.... Whatever this guy supposed to be thinking about. And this guy, he be sitting down there and thinking, and he be thinking about what's happenin' in my life . . . he be deciding on food stamps, and work programs, and the welfare, and the medical aid and the hospitals, whether I be working today. Makin' all kinds a decisions for me. He be worrying about how I spen' my time! Then he lean back in his ol' leather chair, he start thinkin' about da nukular bomb. He be deciding whether I live or die today! Nobody makes those decisions for me. That's for me to decide. I decide when I want to get up in da mornin', when I want to work, when I want to play, when I want to do shit! That's my decision. I'm free. When I die, that's up to God or somebody, not some guy sittin' in a chair. See?

I just wanna live my life. I don't hurt nobody. I turn on the TV set, I see the way everybody be livin'. With their swimming pools and their cars and houses and living room with the fireplace in the living room. . . . There's a fire burnin' in the fireplace, a rug in front of the fireplace. Lady. She be lyin' on the rug, evenin' gown on . . . jewelry, sippin' a glass o' cognac. . . . She be lookin' in the fire, watchin' the branches burnin' up . . . thinkin' about things. Thinkin'. Thinkin'. What's she thinkin' about?

I jus' wanna live my life. I don't ask for too much. I got my room . . . got my bed . . . my chair, my TV set . . . my needle, my spoon, I'm OK, see? I'm OK.

I get up in the mornin' I combs my hair, I wash my face. I go out. I hustle me up a couple a bags a D . . . new works if I can find it.

I take it back to my room, I take that hairwon. I cook it up good in the spoon there. . . . I fill my needle up.

Then I tie my arm (*caressing his arm*) . . . I use a necktie, it's a pretty necktie, my daughter gave it to me. . . . Tie it tight . . . pump my arm . . . then I take the needle, I stick it up into my arm . . . find the hit . . . blood. . . .

Then I undoes the tie . . . I push down on that needle (*pause*) . . . and I got everything any man ever had in the history of this world. Jus' sittin' in my chair. . . .

(*voice lower*) I got love and I got blood. That's all you need. I can feel that blood all going up behind my knees, into my stomach, in my mouth I can taste it....Sometimes it goes back down my arm, come out the hole...stain my shirt....

I know...I know there's people who can't handle it. Maybe I can't handle it. Maybe I'm gonna get all strung out and fucked up....

...Even if I get all strung out and fucked up, don't make no difference to me....Even I get that hepatitis and the broken veins and the ulcers on my arms...addicted. Don't make no difference to me. I was all strung out and fucked up in the first place....

Life is a monkey on my back. You ride aroun' in your car, swim in your warm swimming pool. Watch the fire...I don't mind. I don't mind at all. Just let me have my taste. Have my peace. Just leave me be. Just leave me be.

(turns in toward the dark)

THE LAW

A man walks the stage with a microphone, addressing the audience. He's some sort of preacher.

What has happened to our country? Will somebody answer that question for me, please? We are in trouble. We are in serious trouble. Look around you, what do you see? Crime, perversion, decay, apathy. We are living in a nightmare.

You can't walk down the street for fear of being assaulted. You can't ride in an airplane for fear of being hijacked or blown up. Every corner newsstand openly sells vicious pornography. Every doctor's office is perfectly happy to perform an abortion on you . . . or your daughter. . . . Our children! Our children are subjected daily to the perversions of their schoolteachers and when they come home from school they have nothing better to do than to take drugs or alcohol, watch television, learn how to become homosexuals and rapists. . . .

What a lovely situation, is it not? It is the world we live in today.

In the Bible . . . they tell us of two cities. The worst cities that God had ever seen. They did everything in these cities. They committed every act, natural and unnatural. . . . And God, He looked down on these cities . . . and He saw sin. And He destroyed these cities.

Now you know what cities I'm talkin' about! I'm talkin', of course, about the cities of Sodom and Gomorrah . . . and friends, I regret to inform all of you here tonight...that everything they did in those cities of Sodom and Gomorrah...they do today...they do today. And more. And God destroyed those cities....

Now friends, we have to be honest with ourselves, we have to ask ourselves: "From whence have come these plagues?" And isn't the answer right before our eyes? Do you really have to go to the fountainhead to tell me that the water is poisoned? Well, if you do, go ahead...go into the inner cities. Take a look at the Negroes and the Latins congregating on every street corner....Take a look at the homos and dykes openly strutting up and down the avenues....Take a look at the pimps and prostitutes and the junkies, conspiring with the Jewish slumlords, the Arab bankers and the Italian Mafioso... cutting this country up and destroying it piece by piece!

Don't look to the churches to save you! Don't look to the government to save you! Don't look to the corporations to save you! There's only one place to look for salvation, friends, and that's within yourselves....In your hearts! In your hearts, you know the truth. In your hearts, that's where God is! God's inside your heart, He's a little voice inside you.

When you walk down the street and you see something terrible, you can't believe it and you think to yourself: What a horrible thing! That's the voice of God inside you. When you see something and you think to yourself: How can I stop this? What can I do to stop this? I have to stop this, I have to stop this now! That's the voice of God inside you. I know you have this voice....I know you feel it....We can feel it, we can ALL feel it...deep inside...burning...the truth is burning....

Just as it burned in the heart of Bernie Goetz when he took out that handgun and shot down those Negro subway criminals, he knew the truth. He knew that we are in a war for our souls!...And he who will not protect what is his...is condemned to lose it!

We must continue to put pressure on these Satanic abortion clinics, on these Negro subway criminals, on these Jewish media personalities like Alan Berg, who only understand the discipline of the bullet. These pornographers, like Larry Flynt, who only understand the discipline of the bullet. These homosexual politicians, like Harvey Milk, who only understand the discipline of the bullet. We must show them, we must teach them. God needs our help!

(*He looks the audience in the eyes.*) These people...these people ...these people have sold their souls to the Devil...and if you don't believe me, you go down to Skid Row, take a look at the fallen bodies of the hopeless lost souls, their outstretched filthy hands still trying to reach out and pick up that empty wine bottle! This is the Devil's work right there for you to see! Go down to the red-light district, take a look at some of that porno, take a look at some of those magazines with the young girls on the cover, showing what they should never show anybody, the Devil dancin' in their eyes...these girls are lost! Go down to the city morgue, have 'em show you the dead bodies of the junkies, cold and stiff, lost and forgotten, lying on those metal tables.... These people have no souls....

You go down to the city hospital, you have them show you the AIDS ward...go ahead and take a look...take a good look...and tell me what you see....

This is Satan's work! This is the work of the Devil. The Devil is in the world today! He's sittin' here with us right now. He's sittin' here, and he's laughin'. He's laughin' at us because he seduced us with a life of plenty and he invited us into Hell.

And we all went, didn't we? We took him up on it, didn't we? And we're all goin' down to Hell. . . . You're goin' and you're goin' and you and you! And your children are goin' and your children's babies.

As the blind lead the blind, as the damned lead the damned, onward into oblivion we're goin'. We're goin' down to Hell, unless we do what we know is right! Unless we do what God wants us to do! Unless we do what that little voice inside tells us to do!

If you have to take a bottle, fill it up with gasoline, light it on fire, throw it into one of these abortion clinics, then you do it! If you have to take a handgun, load it up, shoot down one of these black urban barbarians, then you do it! If you have to take a nuclear device and cast it into some country filled with nothing but bearded, terrorist heathens, then you do it.

You do what you have to do! You do what you know is right.

Because this is the world where Satan walks, where Satan walks and where Satan laughs. . . . Where Satan says to himself: "I WON. I BEAT 'EM. I BEAT 'EM ALL."

There's a few of us who don't agree with Mister Satan. There's a few of us who are going to do everything we can, everything within our power . . . to stop him, to do the Lord's work . . .

and make America, and hopefully the rest of the world . . . free of sin . . . again.

Are you with us? Thank you. Amen.

MASTER OF CEREMONIES

A man holding a microphone speaks in a highly modulated "DJ" voice.

Thank you, thank you, thank you....I'm Ricky Rocket from WXXX...and you all know why we're here, you all know what tonight is all about: the last of the Krönenbräu Music Concerts series. And we've saved the best for last! Direct from England, the heaviest of the heavies, more metal to melt your mind: The Molesters! They're gonna come out in just a little while. They're in the back now, strappin' on the leather, strappin' on the metal, polishing their weapons and powdering their noses. They're gonna come out and they're gonna *take you down*. But before they do...one of my favorite bands, one of the hardest-rockin' bands ever to kick ass this side of Nagasaki. Direct from New Jersey...Satan Teens! Ya! Singing their new hit number one this week: "Die Young Die Happy"! They're gonna come out and they're gonna kick your teeth down your throat. But before they do...a band you have to see to believe, a band that makes going to the dentist feel like a party, a band, we don't even know where they come from: Cerebral Hemorrhage! Ya. They're gonna come out and they're gonna blow your mind right out of your skull! TO-NIGHT! LIVE ON THIS STAGE, CEREBRAL HEMORRHAGE, SATAN TEENS AND THE MOLESTERS ARE GOING TO ROCK YOU 'TIL YOUR NOSE BLEEDS! Ya!...But before they do, let me ask you a serious question. Are you feeling good to-night? Are you feeling great tonight? Are you ready to party to-night? Are you ready to be FREE tonight? Break all the boundaries tonight? Are you wasted? Are you wrecked? Are you... FUCKED UP! Ya! I know I am...I know these people down here are feeling pretty good...hey don't party too hardy, it's hard to get the puke off the stage!

Remember, T-shirts and refreshments are on sale at the back of the auditorium and remember, please, from me, Ricky Rocket and all the good guys over at XXX....When you leave tonight...drive safely!

And now, the band that wants to get inside your head... Cerebral Hemorrhage!

(*segue into "air guitar"*)

FRIED-EGG DEAL

A man lies on the floor.

(singing) " . . . We are the world . . . we are the children!"

(rolls over and speaks to someone in the first row of the theater)

Hey there, buddy! How you doin' there, bud? You're my buddy, huh? You got a quarter there for me, bud? You got a quarter for me? Hmmmm?

(standing)

I'm sorry. I'm sorry. I didn't mean to bother you, I'm sorry, I didn't see . . . you're all dressed up . . . you're out for a good time . . . you don't want to be bothered by me. . . .

I'll leave you alone. . . . *(turns, then turns back)* You're here with the little lady, she's a beautiful little lady, you're together . . . you're a together guy . . . GOOD FOR YOU! That's what I say. God bless you, that's what I say! Somebody's gotta make it in this world, it might as well be you, right? Good for you, that's what. . . . I'll leave you, I'll leave . . . I'll get outa here. All right. I'll get outa here.

(turns away, turns back)

See, buddy, people like me. . . . I'm a loser. . . . Always been a loser, always gonna be a loser. I'm a loser, 'cause I'm a drunk. . . . Always been a drunk. When I was a kid, I was a drunk. . . . When I was a baby, I was a baby drunk.

I'm a good-for-nothin' drunken bum, you shouldn't even look at me. Don't even waste your time. Put me in the trash can and flush it, that's what I say. Just get rid of me. . . . Don't even listen to me, OK, bud? I'm sorry, I didn't mean to . . . I just wanna say: "GOOD FOR YOU!"

You work hard, you deserve everything you got . . . 'cause you beat them at their own game . . . you know? 'Cause you know what? They never give you a straight deal in this world . . . never do. You know what they give you in this world? They give you a fried-egg deal. That's what they give you. A fried-egg deal.

You know what I mean, fried-egg deal? (flips his hand) They flip you this way, they flip you that way . . . just like a fried egg, you never know which side you're ending up on. That's the deal, right there. You wake up one morning, you're sunny side up. . . . The next day, you're all scrambled up again, you don't know what's coming next. . . .

And you beat 'em, and I say "GOOD FOR YOU!" Good for you buddy. Me, I'm good for nothin'. I'm good for nothin'. . . . I'll leave you alone. . . .

. . . But you know, I'm good for somethin' buddy. You know why I'm good? I'm . . . good because if . . . if I wasn't where I was . . . you couldn't be where you was . . . 'cause, you know, 'cause (illustrating with his hands flipping) you can't have a top without a bottom. It's impossible. It can't be done. You're on the top and I'm on the bottom. We're like two sides of the same coin. See? And you never know which way that coin's gonna flip.... (*staring at his flipping hand*) You never know which way that coin's gonna go.... That coin there....

(*hand outstretched*) Gotta coin there for me buddy?

(*laughs*)

That's OK, I gotta get goin', I gotta get outa here. It was just a joke, I was just jokin'.... I got a limo waiting for me around the corner, don't want him to wait too long.... Thanks a lot for listenin' to me, buddy, thanks a lot. God bless you.... You're a good guy....

FUN HOUSE

FunHouse premiered at the New York Shakespeare Festival's Public Theater in June 1983, directed by Jo Bonney. That fall Fred Zollo and Frank Gero moved it to the Actor's Playhouse, where it ran for two months.

IN THE DARK

A voice begins in darkness. Slowly lights come up on a man at a table speaking into a microphone.

I wait for dark, the black comes for me. Some people are afraid when the sun goes down. But for me, for me it's good in the deep dark. Warm and dark and close. Some people are afraid of small places, tight spots, restrictive. Not me. I'm in the right place, the good dark place. Like a baby in its womb, like a rat in its hole. . . . I'm OK.

Ever see the black skid marks out on the highway? Ever wonder what happened? I don't. I think about the tires, the rubber . . . the black rubber. Burning. Melting. Pouring down in ropes, in sheets, in long black ribbons all around me. Twisting all around me. Around and around. Black and tight, close and dark. Holding me. Hiding me in the darkness. . . .

Don't you love the smell of black rubber? The way it feels against the skin? Maybe not, it's an acquired taste. Some people never get used to it.

You can work your way up: black leather, then black spandex, then black rubber. Tight. Black. Rubber. Up against you. Pressing. Keeping. Holding. Resilient but firm. Every muscle, every inch is encased in pure black. . . .

The arms, the legs, the chest, the groin, the head. All smooth, all black . . . completely hidden. In my black cocoon I'm where no one can find me, no one can hurt me, no one can touch me. I'm safe in the dark, I'm happy in my hiding place.

I don't have to think, I don't have to feel . . . and the best part is . . . I don't have to see. . . .

INSURANCE

A man is seated at a desk, talking on the phone.

Hello. Suzy? Hi, Suzy, Uncle Freddy. Is Daddy home? . . .
Uncle Freddy. Can you get your daddy, please? . . . Get your father, Susan! Thank you! . . .

Hello, Mr. Stearns, Fred Stanley down at Mutual Insurance!
Sorry to bother you around dinnertime, but I was just going
over your homeowner's policy and I was kind of shocked to
see you don't have very much life insurance. . . . Yes, well, five
thousand dollars isn't very much, Mr. Stearns. *(laughs)* I know
you don't care what happens after you die, but what about
your wife and kids, Mr. Stearns? . . .

Your wife has a job, OK . . . but let's say something should happen and your wife couldn't work? Well, let's say there was a
car accident, you were left fatally injured and your wife paralyzed for life? She wouldn't be able to work then, would she,
Mr. Stearns? Or, let's say you and the missus go to see a play
one night in New York City. You come out of the theater, you
get mugged, a gun goes off, you get a bullet in the brain, you're
left in a coma for months and months and months . . . wife has
to give up her job just to come see you in the hospital. What
would happen then, Mr. Stearns? Have you thought about
that?

Have you thought about cancer, Mr. Stearns? What about cancer? . . . I know you're having dinner right now, but this might

be the most important decision you ever make in your life and I think dinner can wait for five minutes. . . .

Mr. Stearns, I've seen it time and time again: husband dies, wife's left with no pension, no life insurance, she has a mortgage to pay off. . . . You know, of course, Mr. Stearns, most women in this country outlive their husbands. Hundred thousand widows in this country, Mr. Stearns, hundred thousand! . . . What? . . . No, she probably won't get remarried, Mr. Stearns, very few women do. . . .

Mr. Stearns, follow me for just a second, will you? You die, you're dead, you're in the ground! Mrs. Stearns has no pension, no life insurance, she has a mortgage to pay off . . . little Suzy's in the hospital with some kind of rare bone disease. What happens then? Have you thought about that? Have you thought about it? Do you know how many widows are homeless, Mr. Stearns? Do you know how many homeless women become prostitutes, Mr. Stearns?

I'm not saying that, I'm not saying that, Mr. Stearns. I'm just saying that I know you're a loving father and husband and you only want the best for little Suzy and . . . uh, right! Right! Edwina. Lovely name Edwina . . . and you'd hate to leave Edwina and Suzy unprotected in this terrible and frightening and— let's be honest with each other, Mr. Stearn—perverse and disturbed world we live in today. . . . Why, I could show you street corners in New York where little girls no more than fifteen years old sell themselves . . . and their mothers standing right next to them. . . .

Yes, oh . . . ummm, well, ha ha . . . oh, I'd say around two hundred and fifty thousand dollars' worth would do the trick. . . .

Easy terms . . . easy terms, we'll work something out, don't worry. . . . When can you come by? . . . Tomorrow? Tomorrow I'll be here all day. Eleven o'clock? That would be great, Mr. Stearns, I'll see you tomor—what? Oh, don't worry about the cost, we'll talk about that tomorrow. . . . Look, Mr. Stearns, get back to your roast-beef dinner . . . and say hi to, uh, Edwina for me. And Mr. Stearns? . . .

. . . Take care! (hangs up)

INSIDE

A man standing with a microphone speaks in a singsong voice.

OK, gentlemen, this is it, what you've been waiting for, right through that door. Inside, inside! All your dreams come true, don't be blue, this is it, check it out! I said don't wait, don't hesitate. Run don't walk, show's about to start! See it, feel it! Live, living, real. In full color, completely open, fully revealed, "X"-posed for your eyes only! A house of dreams, your very own *Fantasy Island*. If it turns you on, we got it: black, white, red and yellow, boys and girls at your disposal. Men and women behind closed doors! Until you are satisfied! Check it out! Just for you, just the way you want it. You can't do better, nobody offers more. Now, now, now, now, now! No tricks, no substitutions, it's the real thing. A mental orgy, an experience! For you, for them. Lose yourself, immerse yourself in the delirium of total abandon. All the way, all you ever wanted, all you can take! Inside, inside, come right inside and get it. Get it hot! Get it now! Dreams, dreams, dreams, dreams, dreams. . . .

SHIT, FUCK, PISS

A bent and craggy man, a Bowery Lear, rails at the storm of filth he lives in.

Fuckin' yer shit, fuck, piss, yer shit, fuck, piss, ya shifugpiss!

What's that!? (*points at floor*) What's that!?!

(*picks up a tiny speck of rubbish on the stage*) It's shit, that's what it is! There's shit on the ground, shit in the air. . . . It's all a bunch of shit if you ask me.

(*to audience*) You know what I'm talking about! You know what I'm talking about! We're living in a cesspool is what I'm talking about. A human trash heap. Everywhere you go there's piles of filth, piles of garbage. You have to step in shit, step in the garbage. In the pools of piss, the streams of piss! The rivers! The rivers are polluted! And the oceans? The oceans are full of dead fish. Dead fish and oil slicks!

And the dead fish wash up on the beaches, see? And then the rats come and they eat the dead fish. And then the cats come and they eat the rats . . . and then the dogs come and they eat the cats . . . and then the dogs, you know what the dogs do? The dogs, they shit all over the place! That's what they do!

Dog shit and horse shit . . . pigeon shit! (*looks up as he steps backward into an imaginary pile*) Shit, fuck, piss! (*scrapes foot on table edge*) We're living in a toilet, that's what we're doing! Turds in the toilet! I say flush the toilet! FLUSH THE TOILET! FLUSH THE TOILET!

THE SPECIALIST

A man stands and talks in a straightforward manner to the audience.

The first piece of equipment you want to make sure you have on hand is a nice big bucket...around so big, so deep. (*indicates with hands*)...Just fill that up with water. Nice and deep. Right up to the brim. Take your subject by the back of the neck. Firm grip. Bring him over to the bucket...and push his head right under the water. Baptize him. Put the fear of God into him....Soak 'im good.

Then up...then back down again....Fifteen, twenty seconds is good. Just watch the air bubbles. Air bubbles stop, give it around five more seconds....And back down. Make sure you have a firm grip, sometimes they buck a little. And stay out of the way of the legs, they kick too....Now you have a subject you're ready to work with: he's wet, he's tired and he's scared.

The next piece of equipment you want to have on hand is a nice big metal worktable about so wide, so deep. (*indicates with hands*)...I suggest metal just because it lasts longer. Nice big working surface....Get your subject up onto the worktable, strap down the arms, the legs, the head. Piece of gaffer's tape, duct tape, over the mouth and you have him where you want him. Just pinch the nostrils and he can't breathe. He's completely at your disposal. Fingertip control.

OK. So how do we begin? Myself, I like to start with a simple psychological device, kind of a trademark of mine. I'm a smoker, OK? Bad habit, I know I should quit. Anyway, I like to just take the cigarette out, everybody's afraid of fire, take the cigarette out (*indicates with his cigarette*) and just push it right into the navel, soft like wax.... Oh, it hurts. It hurts.... I'm sure any of you who were in Nam or Korea came across this baby once or twice. Just leave it in there. Kind of an hors d'oeuvre.

What do we want to do for the main course? Well, some people like to work with rubber truncheons, knitting needles, plastic bags over the head, breaking fingers, twisting arms. *Hey!* We're not in the Dark Ages. We have electricity. Electricity when properly applied will achieve whatever ends you desire. Simply take your two electrodes, nothing more than a couple of bare wires hooked up to a generator.

Just take the two wires and press them firmly up against the palms of the hands, the soles of the feet, inside the ear, the eyelids, the nostrils, lips, gums . . . of course, any cavities or fillings you may find.... The armpits, the nipples, the genitalia. All very effective. Of course, I know a lot of you have worked with electricity before. So I won't go into a lot of detail.

However, one point I always stress whenever I'm talking about electricity to training groups such as this is that you have a licensed physician on hand, a medical doctor. For two reasons: First of all, he can tell you exactly how much electricity is needed to get the job done. That's his area of expertise, his job. Use him, ask him questions. Secondly, you have a lot of people working around the area, around the electricity. You don't want anyone to get hurt.

We'll finish up the seminar tomorrow evening. Until then, if you have any questions, please talk to your commanding officer.

(*A phone rings. He answers it.*)

STARVING CHILDREN

A man strides around the stage with evangelical purpose, addressing the audience with a microphone.

WHAT ARE YOU AFRAID OF?...What are you afraid of?... The only thing you have to fear is fear itself....

So many people write to me, they write to the station, they stop me in the street, they call me on the telephone. They call me and they say: "Reverend Tim...Reverend Tim, I have a problem. My husband's out of work and he's been drinking." "Reverend Tim, I have a problem. My daughter crashed the car up and I think maybe she lost her virginity...." "Reverend Tim, I got no job...." "Reverend Tim, I got no money...." "Reverend Tim, I'm sick...." Problems, problems, problems! And people write to me about them.

I got a letter the other day from a Mrs. R in Seattle that I would like to share with you right now. Mrs. R has a problem that I would like to share with you because I think it tells us so much about how God can help each and every one of us. She wrote me and she said:

"Reverend Tim, I watch your show every day and you are an inspiration to me, Reverend Tim....But Reverend Tim, I have a problem: Ten years ago my boy got back from Vietnam and he was missing a leg. And ever since that time he's been down and lonely and depressed. And now, Reverend Tim, I think he's using heroin, Reverend Tim. And the other day he went out and bought a shotgun, Reverend Tim, and I'm afraid he might gonna hurt somebody, Reverend Tim, maybe he's gonna kill somebody, Reverend Tim! Maybe he's gonna kill himself, Reverend Tim. Reverend Tim, I'm afraid! Reverend Tim. I'm scared! I'm afraid, I'm scared!..."

I read that letter...and I got a little angry...because I thought to myself...Where is the faith? WHERE IS THE FAITH!?! You know we are God's children, we are His sheep. God is our teacher. He's up there to lead us, to help us. God is just settin' up in heaven every day just thinking up new ways to teach us, new ways to test us, new ways to SHOW US HIS LOVE! He just sits up there all day long thinking (He's got nothing better to do). He just says to Himself: "Now what kind of obstacle can I put in their path today that will lead 'em on the right road? What kind of weight can I put on their shoulder that will teach 'em a thing or two?"

(Tim indicates dropping heavy weights on a tiny individual standing next to him.) "How's he doing with that? Hmmmm, maybe a little bit more? Just a little bit more...."

AS IT SAYS IN THE BIBLE: "HE WHO CARRIES THE GREATEST BURDEN, HE SHALL KNOW THE GREATEST TRUTH!" Now think about that for a second....It also says: "God helps him who helps himself!"

(Addressing the camera over the audience) Mrs. R, sure times are tough, sure life is difficult. Sure you got "problems": your boy's handicapped, he's on drugs, maybe he's gonna kill himself...maybe he's gonna kill you...but Mrs. R...if you've got FAITH. If you've got WILLPOWER...you can make it.... I know you can. (to the audience) I know we all can.

(*pause*)

Well, so much for our petty personal problems. . . .

I would like to talk to you right now about some little children who carry a burden much greater than any we'll ever know. I'm talking, of course, about the millions upon millions of starving little children in Southeast Asia, in Africa, in South America. Millions upon millions of starving little children.

(*to the camera*) If you're watching at home you can see pictures of them on your TV set. (*to the audience*) Those of you in our audience here can see them up in the monitors. Look at 'em all you want. Aren't they cute? They're starving . . . and they're little.

I want you to think about those starving little children for just a minute. And then I want you to think about that extra piece of pie you had with dinner last night. You weren't even hungry and you had to have that second helping of pie. That extra slice of pie! . . . I want you to think about that MOVIE you went to see, filled with sex and violence. What did it cost you? Five dollars and who knows how much for the hot buttered popcorn! I want you to think about that popcorn. I want you to think about that slice of pie!

. . . And then I want you to think about those little, starving children. And I want you . . . to take out your checkbook . . . and I want you to write me . . . a check for eighteen dollars. And next month I want you to write me another check. And the month after that and the month after that. . . . Eighteen dollars a month! And you'll be doing everything you can . . . everything you possibly can . . . to help ME do everything I can...to help those millions upon millions of starving...little...children!

Eighteen dollars a month, and you can end starvation in the whole world today. Eighteen dollars a month, and the next time you want an extra slice of pie, just go ahead and eat all you want! The next time you see some poor beggar on the street with his hand up to you begging for a dime, begging for a quarter...you can walk on by with a clear conscience 'cause you sent me eighteen bucks!...The next time you see some starvin' little baby on the TV set, all withered and bony, with his little stomach stickin' out, you can look all you want and say to yourself: "It's not my fault!"

You know, there are two kinds of people in the world: the haves and the have-nots....And among the haves, there are two kinds of haves: there are those who take out the checkbook, and then there are those who just turn off the TV....

Which one are you?

SITCOM

A man picks up the phone at a table, answering in a shrill, fast-talking voice.

Arnie! Arnie! Yeah, yeah, listen. Sid! You got two minutes? Yeah, yeah, listen, I got a great idea for a sitcom . . . sitcom, Arnie, sitcom! Situation comedy, what are you doing up there in your office, take the straw outa ya nose for two minutes and listen to me for a second. Arnie! Arnie! Concentrate! Follow me.

Scenario: New York City! Apartment building in New York. Black guy lives in the apartment. Nice black guy, middle-class black guy, button-down-sweater type of guy, smokes a pipe. Yeah, yeah . . . harmless black guy. Benson! Benson! We got Benson in this apartment. . . . Across the hall from him, para-plegic kid in a wheelchair. . . . Huh? You don't need a real one, you just get any cute kid and stick him in a wheelchair. What? Fuck the unions! The kid's in a wheelchair here, black guy across the hall. They got a real nice relationship here. Big brother, interracial kind of thing. Yeah. Mushy liberal stuff . . . a show with meaning. . . . Yeah, a show with relevance to the social problems of today. . . . yeah, yeah, *Mary Tyler Moore, Hill Street, M*A*S*H, Cosby, The Waltons!*

Wait, wait, more! Top floor of the building we got a whore-house! Hookers going up and down the stairs all time of night and day. Falling over the kid with the wheelchair, sticking lollipops in his mouth, patting his head. Cute stuff like that, sweet stuff, light humor, family humor. . . . Ground floor of the apartment building: gay health club! Homos working out with weights, building up the pectoral muscles. . . . See what I'm saying? We got the beefcake down here doing sit-ups while the cheesecake's up here doing push-ups! Something for everybody! Wait, wait, one more apartment, teen-age kid living with his mother, OK, this is the humor of the show. Kid wants to kill everybody in New York City! One week he makes an atom bomb in his bedroom, next week he puts LSD in the city water supply, then he derails a subway car, who knows? Crazy stuff, funny stuff, hilarious stuff! We'll call the show *Upstairs, Downstairs*. . . . Huh? Who's PBS? Fuck PBS! . . . Those are little people. They don't count. We'll buy the title off of them. . . . Arnie, what are you busting my balls about this thing for? Yeah? That was two years ago! Yeah, I know what's good for me. What's good for me is what's good for you! Arnie, we'll have lunch next week and discuss the project, OK? Huh? Look Arnie, I got a call on the other line, I got to get off. . . . Arnie, I'm getting off. . . . Arnie? . . . Yes, I love you, but I'm getting off. . . . I'm getting off, Arnie! Arnie . . . Arnie . . . Arnie. . . . Good-bye! (*hangs up*)

CALAMARI

A man sits at a table, speaks in a growly, inner-city voice.

Every time I have fried calamari, I feel like I'm gonna blow up!...Vincent, be a good boy and pour your uncle a cup of coffee there....Just a half a cup, no sugar, I'm having a diet....

So Vincent, you go visit Frank in the hospital? How's he doing, he's doing OK, right? Just gallstones, right? I was gonna go visit him last week but I got home from work and I couldn't move! I even bought him a geranium for his room there, but I left it on the Mister Coffee machine in the office and it got all burnt up!

So how's he doing? He's doing all right, huh? Just gallstones, huh? Gallstones is nothing! I saw the whole operation on *Marcus Welby*, M.D. Right on TV they showed it. Very simple operation, I could do it myself. They just make a little cut in the stomach like this . . . then they got this thing, uh like, it's like a grapefruit spoon, OK? They take this grapefruit spoon and they dig out those gallstones. That's all . . . and then they throw 'em away. Throw 'em away right in the garbage. They don't even keep 'em. You figure for the amount of money you pay for that operation they'd at least give you the gallstones to take home . . . show 'em to the kids . . . give 'em to the dog to play with. . . . Forgetaboutit! . . . Merv Griffin had those gallstones one time, he was back on the show in two weeks.

Gallstones is nothing. Of course, when Frank went in, he thought he was gonna DIE! First he thinks he's got appendicitis, then he thinks he's got a heart attack. Then, then they tell him he might be gettin' cancer! And with his mother passing away last year cancer and his brother two years ago cancer! Everybody in that family's dying of cancer! Even the dog died. Remember that little dog they used ta have? The poodle? What was his name there? That cute dog? What was—?

(interrupting himself, shouting to the back of the stage)

ANGLE! ANGIE!...WHAT WAS THE NAME OF FRANK'S DOG? *(pause)* YEAH, THE ONE THAT DIED! *(longer pause)*... Snowball! Snowball! That was it, remember little Snowball? Little pink poodle, they used to dye him all pink, remember that? Lick ya hand? Yeah, he died....

Listen, Vincent, let me have a little piece of that pie there, will you please? Yeah, just a thin piece. Just a thin...well, bigger than that for crying out loud, what are you trying to do, starve me to death, come on!...And put some whipped cream on top!...I don't know what it is, I can't eat a piece of pie without whipped cream it....It just doesn't taste right. I think you need the cream to lubricate the crumbs, make 'em go down smoother.

Thank you....Huh?...What operation? I didn't have no operation. That was an "exploratory," Vincent! An exploratory is not an operation. Exploratory they just open you up, look around inside and close you up again. They don't change nothing. They said I was in perfect health. All I have is a little benign tumor....No, Vincent! Benign! You're thinking of a *malignant* tumor. Malignant and benign are two different things. Look, malignant tumors are very, very bad for you. But benign tumors . . . benign tumors . . . you can have all the benign tumors you want, they don't hurt ya . . . they're good for ya.

What are you going to do about it anyway? Everybody gets cancer these days, it's in the food you eat, it's in the water you drink . . . that disoksin stuff and the DDT, and the PCB and the acid rain. Every day they think of some new thing put in the food, gives you cancer.

You know, Vincent, it wasn't like this when we was kids! We didn't have all this poison in everything you eat and drink all over the place. . . . Take asbestos. When we was kids we used to have asbestos all over the place. Nobody ever died from asbestos. We used to play in asbestos! Nowadays, nowadays you go down to the drugstore to buy yourself some aspirin, some Tylenol, and some maniac put cyanide in the bottle! You take it home and you drop dead! Buy yourself some baby food, it's got ground glass in it! You don't know what you're eatin' anymore. . . .

And if you don't eat nothin', you don't eat nothin', you get that starvation disease . . . uh, you know . . . that starvation disease . . . they uh . . . (shouts again back over his shoulder) ANGIE! ANGIE! . . . Well, turn the water off for crying out loud, I gotta ask you an important question! . . . What's she doing in there, washing the dishes twenty-four hours a day! . . . WHAT WAS THE NAME OF THE DISEASE THAT KAREN CARPENTER GIRL DIED FROM? . . . IT WAS IN THE PEOPLE MAGAZINE. . . . THE ONE IN THE BATHROOM! . . . YEAH. . . . The anorexia, you get the anorexia! See what I'm saying, Vincent? If you eat you die and if you don't eat you die! I'd rather eat.

Huh? No, I'm not going, I'm not going. Look, I went to the wake, I went to the funeral, enough of these social functions. I mean, Louie was a nice guy and everything, but all we're gonna do is go over to that house and sit around with Mary and talk and eat and besides all Mary's got is a black-and-white TV set! Louie was too cheap when he was alive to buy a color TV and now look what's happened! Mary's stuck with black-and-white for the rest of her life!

Besides, there's a show on TV I want to watch that night. . . . A Charles Bronson movie . . . uh, you know the one . . . the good one, where he's got that big gun and he goes all over New York City and kills all those Puerto Ricans. . . . Yeah, it's a good movie. . . . Nah, I got it on the cable TV, on the cable.

You know what they say, Vince. When you got cable TV you never got to go out. What do I got to go out for? I got everything I need right here: my color TV set, hundred and five stations; my own sofa, nice and soft; my own kitchen, plenty of food in the icebox; my own bathroom, plenty of toilet paper. What do I gotta go out for? Stay home, it's safer, it's cleaner, it's more sanitary. Stay in the house, lock the door, piece of Sara Lee cake, turn on the TV. That's livin'. What else you want from life?

Plus, I just got the videotape machine. Yeah, it's in the bedroom, come on, I'll show it to ya. You can watch whatever you wanna watch whenever you wanna watch it. (*stands*) Like last week Ronald Reagan was on TV, gave that big speech? I recorded the whole thing on my videotape machine! Anytime I wanna watch Ronald Reagan, anytime at all, day or night, middle of the night, BANG! (*hits table*) Ronald Reagan on TV! You can't beat it!

Plus Angie's got that Jane Fonda exercise tape, you know the one? . . . What, me? Forget about it. I'll tell you something though, that Jane Fonda, I wouldn't kick her outa bed! Uh???? (*He starts laughing as he turns to exit. The laughter turns into racking coughs. . . .*)

MAKE YOURSELF NEW

A bright-eyed, cheery, energetic fellow runs onto the stage.

Hey, how we all doing today? Good? Great!!! Let's all make to-day a great day! Let's WORK at it! Remember, today's the first day of the rest of your life! If you want something bad enough, you can have it . . . all you have to do is . . . (*throws a wide-arcing fist*) GIVE IT ALL YOU GOT!!!

So are we UP? Are we POSITIVE? Are we ready to CHANGE OUR LIVES? OK! Let's go! (*points to sound booth*) Music, maestro!

(*disco beat starts up, to which he exercises, while shouting to the audience*) Let's start with the bosoms, shall we? Lift and separate. . . . (*limp arm exercises*) . . . And one and two and make yourself new, three and four and do it some more! Only helps if it hurts! And jumping jacks! . . . One and two, if Jane can do it, so can you . . . three and four, burn, baby, burn! Work those thunder thighs . . . you made 'em, you get rid of 'em! . . . And kick, kick, kick, kick. . . . How we doin' with our diets, huh girls? Yogurt (*kick*), grapefruit (*kick*), cottage (*kick*) cheese (*kick*). . . .

Come on, you can do it! CHANGE YOUR LIVES! Come on, it's FUN! (*He kicks a few more times, obviously under a strain.*) Now stretch, stretch, stretch, stretch . . . oh, can you feel that new "you" coming out? (*voice is strained*) I CAN! . . . Sit-ups!!! Time to make your tummy tiny! (*He collapses to the floor.*) One and two and make yourself new. . . .

COLLEGE OF CASHIER EDUCATION

A smooth-talking, Hispanic disco radio DJ (over sound system).

Hey, you're listening to Roco, the voice of disco on WFRO in New York City. . . . Let me ask you something: how would you like to earn that big kind of money, huh? Pay all your bills. How would you like to drive a big car, ride in a jet plane? All you gotta do is call the College of Cashier Education! That's right, the College of Cashier Education. Listen to this: You can be a real cashier. Just call CCE and in two weeks you can be cashing in! They teach you everything you need to know, you know? And there's a lot of jobs for cashiers: boutique jobs, supermarket jobs, restaurants, beauty parlors. That's right. Get rid of all your money problems. . . . And if you're a handicapped veteran, don't forget about their special handicapped veteran program. If you served your country and you got trouble getting around, this is the job for you! So get on the phone right now and call the College of Cashier Education at 555-CASH. Tell 'em Roco sent you. . . . OK, hey, I hope you're all hot and ready for some hot disco dancing 'cause we got the hits for you tonight! I know the girls are hot because I feel hot and when I feel hot everything I touch gets hot. . . . *(fade out)*

HONEY, I'M HOME!

A man is lying on the floor, singing in a raunchy voice.

God bless America! Land that I love! Stand beside her...and guide her (*pause*) blah, blah, blah, blah, blah, blah, blah, blah! (*He starts coughing, turns onto his side and notices bystander.*)

Hey! Hey buddy, can you give me a hand here? I just slipped and fell down for a second, could you help me out please? Buddy, pal? How about helping out an old veteran! I served in Korea, buddy! I helped save this country from communism, whaddya say? "Ask not what your country can do for you... ask what you can do for your country...."

Remember that one? JFK said that.... They blew *his* brains out!

Hey buddy, what do you say? Am I invisible or something? What, am I talking to the fire hydrant here? You! Mister! The guy with the *New York Times* under his arm, how about it? It'll only take you a second.... What's a matter, afraid you're gonna miss your bus to Connecticut??? What, do you have to rush home and skim the pool, is that it? Drive the wife to the Amnesty International meeting? Is that why you can't help me up here for a second?

I know you can hear me! I know you can hear me! Don't act like you can't hear me, buddy! I know all about guys like you! Guys like you don't give a fuck about nobody, do ya? Do ya? You're just a bunch of bums, aren't ya? No good to nobody.... You think you're something special 'cause you got a

Gold American Express card...and 'cause you drink "fine wines."...Well, I drink wine too, buddy, nothing special about that!...

What are you gonna do? Go home now and have a nice little dinner with the wife and the kids and the dog and gerbil?!? Nice little roast-beef dinner, is that what you're gonna have? Roast beef and gravy??? And little baked potatoes....Maybe some little...asparagus tips! Nice little asparagus tips....Is that what you're gonna have tonight? Is that why you can't pick me up? Because you're gonna have asparagus tips tonight?????

(He begins to get to his feet, very shakily.) I know all about guys like you! With your London Fog raincoat! And the briefcase that your wife gave you for Christmas with your initials on it and the combination lock! (pause) What do you need a combination lock for, you a secret agent or something?

You're all the same, you go home, you walk in the front door and you all say the same damn thing:

(He's standing now, mimicking the man...in a hoarse voice.) Honey, I'm home! Honey, I'm home! Honey, I'm home!

THE PACER

A man paces and stops, paces and stops, throughout the monologue, talking to himself. He speaks to the audience more directly as the monologue goes on.

Yeah, yeah, yeah, yeah, they're always telling you the same old story, always giving you the same old story: one plus one equals two, two plus two equals four, you reap what you sow. It always starts the same way, it always ends the same way. . . . I don't, I don't, I don't got any answers. . . . I don't know what the answer is. . . .

You're coming and you're going, you're coming and you're going, you take it or you leave it. You make it or you need it. It's human nature, it's human nature, the same old story: man against man, man against nature, man against himself!

Beginning, middle, end. Climax . . . anticlimax. . . . Subplot! . . . But you gotta read between the lines . . . you can't win the way things are now. Oh, yeah, sure, sure, sure, sure, sure it used to be all different. Sure when I was a kid, when I was a kid everything was different: Bread, ten cents a loaf. Eggs, fifty cents. No plastic bags. No plastic bags! NO PLASTIC BAGS! Waxed paper! No pollution, no conspiracy.

Everything was different. Easy to understand. I can't understand. . . . I can't, I can't, I can't make any sense out of it. And then the guy, the guy, the guy, the guy says, "Get out of here!" "Get out of here!" . . . "You get out of here," that's what I should of said to him! "You get out of here!" I got no place to go! No place to go! It's crazy, it's a madhouse, a funhouse. . . .

It's dog-eat-dog, man-eat-man, eat or be eaten, hunt or be hunted! It's the letter of the law, the law of the land and the land is jungle!...You see what I'm saying, you follow what I'm talking about??? Now, now look, look, look, look....I gotta look after myself first. They want you to give to the taxes, give to the starving children, the abandoned babies, the blind people, the poor people!

I can't worry about those poor people! I gotta worry about me first!...And then, then they say, "Don't worry about it! Don't worry about it! We'll take care of you. Everything's gonna be all right! Everything's gonna be terrific! We got a safety net for you! A safety net for you! Jump in the safety net! Go ahead, jump in the safety net....Go ahead, jump. And here's some free cheese to go with you...and here's a space shuttle!"...I don't want no space shuttle! I just want a cup of coffee!

...I give up, I'm gonna give it up! It's just gettin' harder and harder, every day, day in, day out...you gotta stand in line, you gotta stand in line for hours and hours and hours....And then you get to the end of the line, you get to the end of the line and they say, "No more!" "No more! We don't got no more for you!...No more for you!" For who? For who? Who's gettin' it? Who's gettin' it? I'm not! I'm not gettin' it!

You're either winnin' or you're losin', you're either sinkin' or you're swimmin'...and I'm sinkin', see! I'm in a little life-boat with no oars and I'm sinkin' in the ocean....

(indicates with posture) I'm on a little piece of ice, just gettin' smaller and smaller and smaller day by day by day, goin' into the water...and that water's polluted, it's dirty, it's disgusting...and I can't swim! I can't swim!

Sink or swim, fish or cut bait! You're either part of the problem or you're part of the solution. . . . And what's the solution? What's the solution? The bomb? The bomb? Drop the bomb. Go ahead, drop it! I don't care! I'm not waiting for any packages! I got no all-paid vacation coming up! I'm no Little Orphan Annie. (*sings in a cracked voice*) "Tomorrow! Tomorrow! Tomorrow!" . . . Where's the tomorrow? You know where tomorrow is? You got a tomorrow? I don't got no tomorrow. . . . OH!!! I know what you're gonna say now. . . . More! More! Tomorrow is more . . . that's what tomorrow is. . . . More money. We make more money, everything will be all right, that's it. Let's all make some more money . . . all go to work and make more money . . . and then we can make more kids . . . more people, we need a lot more people! What do we need more people for? What's wrong with me ?

More people, more radio stations, we need a lot more radio stations . . . and TV stations, we gotta have more TV stations! Lots more TV stations . . . UHF, VHF, cable TV, satellite TV, mini, maxi, tape deck, PBS, CBS. . . .

(*A loud voice-over of a rock radio DJ comes over the sound system, getting louder and louder.*)

"Hey, this is John Cummings on WXXX, the home of HEAVY METAL! I'm gonna give away ten thousand dollars in the next hour . . . ten thousand dollars in our MADNESS contest. Bet you could use that money, huh? Well, who knows, maybe you'll win! On the other hand, maybe you won't. (*laughs*) Then you'll just have to SUFFER! And while you're burning in your own private hell, we've got the new AC/DC album for ya right here at WXXX, twenty-four hours a day ROCK-AND-ROLLLLLLL" (*music begins*)

. . . It never stops, day in, day out. In the subway, the kids with their boxes: *Boom, boom, boom!* In the supermarket, they never shut it off. In the streets. In the elevators. The noise. It never stops. What are they talking about? In my apartment, the people upstairs, always playing that music! (*shouts to the people*) Hey! Turn it down. Hey! I'm trying to think down here! Hey come on!

(*Pacer goes into mad dance which segues into an "air guitar" dance.*)

SHINING STAR

A man is sitting at a table, leaning forward and speaking into a microphone. His hands are behind his back. Perhaps he is handcuffed. He is lit by a single instrument shining directly into his eyes.

Yeah, yeah, yeah, yeah. . . . I got something to say. I got a few "last words." This is what I got to say: You don't know. You don't know anything about me, you don't know anything about the world, about reality, got it? I mean, who the hell are you people? Who are you to say, "He dies"? What gives you that right? My "peers"? My "jury of peers"? You're not my peers, 'cause I look down on you. You and your fat-ass existence. You and your TV brains. You never been anywhere, you don't know nothin'. . . . All you know is what some idiot on the boob tube tells you.

So maybe I killed those girls . . . so what? I didn't. But what if I did? Insignificant people die all the time. You don't seem to be too concerned when there's a war going on or there's children starving in Africa. What about that, huh? You're responsible for that and you're responsible for putting me away! I mean, first of all, I'm innocent, OK? But second of all, I'm somebody 'cause I have seen the world. I have been in the desert, man, I have seen the "shining star." I have rode with the Kings, man, and I have rode with the best!

I know what the truth is, and the truth is that I count and you don't. It's like when you're a little kid and you step on ants on the sidewalk. You know they don't count. Well, it's the same with me. You're just a bunch of ants. You're not even alive as far as I know. You could just be a bunch of robots. You might be robots filled with blood and guts but you're still robots, see?

See, I can see that. . . . I understand that. 'Cause I have seen the shining star in the desert, man. I have rode a Harley at a hundred and fifty miles per hour and I have seen reality go by! I have been through it. I have tripped in places you don't even know exist! I have shot dope in the Mekong, man. I have looked death right in the eyes, and I saw the Stars and Stripes!

And no one can dispute me! Those who have tried are very sorry now. They're not around to talk about it. 'Cause I'm always ready. . . . There's a war comin' on and this is only the beginning. Only the strong will survive. It's gonna be kill-or-be-killed. Hand to hand. Mind to mind. And I'm ready, see? I'm ready for anything, anything. I passed every test.

See, I will survive 'cause it all passes through me. It's up to me to hold it all together. I am the center. It's like cosmic. Like oriental. You got to go all the way out and come all the way back and keep your center. Like if there was a candle here right now, I could put my hand over it and I wouldn't get burned. I wouldn't. I wouldn't feel any pain at all. 'Cause I can take it, see. I'm just testin' myself harder and harder, goin' out further and further to the shining star. . . .

You people, you people livin' out your safe protected little lives. You think you know about things? You think you can tell me about things? You can't tell me about nothing, man, 'cause I have seen it all. I have shook hands with the devil!

And you wanna come here and you wanna fight with me and you will lose man, you will lose! 'Cause I am the stronger one, and the stronger one always wins, that's the law of the jungle. That's survival of the fittest. And I am the stronger. I am the stronger physically, mentally and spiritually.... (*laughs to himself*)

See, that's the big joke, see? You're just here 'cause I'm here! You just came here tonight to see me! I'm the one! I'm sittin' up here, and you're just sittin' out there scared: "There's the killer. We gotta kill the killer." You're afraid of me, like Jesus! And you think you can just put me away and that's the end of it and that's where you're wrong, man! You can't get rid of me!

'Cause I'm everywhere! I'm in the air, I'm in the ground, I'm inside you. See, 'cause the shining star, it doesn't go away. It's always there in my brain, burnin', shinin' in my head.... And when everything's gone, when everything is blowed away . . . I'll still be here!

(*fade to black*)

MEN INSIDE

Men Inside was first seen at Franklin Furnace in New York City in February 1981 and "premiered" at the New York Shakespeare Festival's Public Theater in July 1982.

FREAKSHOW

Ladies and gentlemen! Step right up and see the freaks. The freak show is about to begin. . . .

Twenty-five cents, two bits, one-fourth of a dollar. . . .

Right behind this curtain, ladies and gentlemen, step right up, come as close as you like, examine them to your heart's content. . . .

See the Fat Lady, the fattest woman in the world! Weigh her on our scales and be amazed! She's huge, a veritable Leviathan!

See the Snake Boy with scalelike skin, there's nothing like him, the eighth wonder of the world!

The Deaf, Dumb and Blind Man, watch him stumble, watch him fall! Fun for the whole family.

The He-She! Is it a man? Is it a woman? Only you can decide!

See the pimply dwarf commit acts unspeakable! Watch him dance with a poodle!

Once in a hundred years, a Negro and a Chinaman mate and we have the Offspring, right behind this curtain, ladies and gentlemen, a medical impossibility.

Yes! Yes! And for the same price, tonight only see Doctor Cyclops, the one-eyed man. He'll give you the cold stare!

And his friend, the Legless Wonder. He's got wheels instead of legs, wheels instead of legs. A one-man roller derby.

And finally, for the first time in captivity, not an imitation, not a duplication, but the real thing. A genuine, homosexual Siamese twin.

Step right up, ladies and gentlemen, step right up. The freak show's about to begin!

SUPERMAN!

Little boy leaps off a table, pretending to fly.

SUPERMAN! Duh-duh-duh duh-duh-duh-duh-duh-duh-duh! (*to the Superman theme song*)

Pssssssshhhhhhhh!!!!!

Hi Dad! I was just practicing my Superman, Dad!

Am I doin' it right, Dad? Am I doin' it right? Hey Dad, guess what I did today? I ran as fast as I could and I threw a rock at a bird and I killed it!

Pretty good, huh Dad?

Hey Dad, when I grow up I'm gonna be just like you, huh Dad? I'm gonna be tall and strong and never make any mistakes and drink beer and shave and drive a car and get a check. I'm gonna be just like you, huh Dad?

Dad, can I ask you a question?

When I grow up I'm not gonna be poor, am I Dad?

Am I?

I'm not gonna be a poor old bum on the street. All smelly and living in a box, am I Dad? I'm gonna be rich like you, huh Dad?

And...Dad? I'm...I'm not gonna be a alcoholic, am I Dad? Like Mr. Johnson down the street, never cuts the lawn. I'm not gonna be an alcoholic with a big red nose and throwing up.

And I'm not gonna be a junkie either, am I Dad? Like on *Kojak*. And not have a life worth living and OD all the time. I'm not gonna OD, huh Dad, huh?

Dad? Joey says I'm gonna be a homo! I'm not gonna be a homo, am I Dad? *Homo!* We're not homos, are we Dad?

Dad? NO WAY I CAN BE A NIGGER, HUH DAD, HUH? 'Cause you're not a nigger and Mom's not a nigger, huh? Huh? HUH? We're American, huh Dad?

Dad? I got one more question. When I grow up...I'm...I'm not...gonna...gonna go...I'm... (*begins stuttering and falls to the floor in a fit*)

NICE SHOES

Very friendly, but with growing menace.

Hey...hey...you...you with the glasses. Come here. Come here for a second, I wanna ask you a question....No come here. I never seen you around the neighborhood before and I just want ta meet ya....What's ya name?...Mike? Michael... Mike. How ya doin' there, Mike? I'm Sonny, this here's Joey and this is Richie. He's a big guy, huh?

...Hey...hey...hold on for a second, Mike, don't walk away from me when I'm talking to you....Uh...I just saw you walkin' around here and uh, I never seen youse before and you're wearing all these nice clothes—Joey! Lookit dis guy's clothes...nice clothes....I like the clothes....These are the kind a clothes you wanna be wearin', Joey....Bet you got these clothes up Bloomingdale's didnja?

And the shoes! Nice shoes! I like those shoes, huh? Richie, check out Mike's shoes....I like those shoes, Mike....Hey! You know what we call shoes like dose? "C-Shoes," "C-Shoes."...You wanna know why?...'Cause dey cost a C-note...hundred bucks, get it?

(Laughing, he turns to Joey.) Pretty funny...C-shoes, huh?... *(whips around, noticing Mike getting away)*

Hey-hey-hey-hey-hey....Mike, don't walk away from me when I'm talkin' to you here now! That's very impolite, you know? You're being impolite to me...and you're embarrassing me in front of my friends. . . . You're insulting me in front of my friends . . . and when somebody insults me I get angry. . . . I get angry and I hurt people . . . heh heh.

RICHIE, SHUT UP! SHUT YA FUCKIN' MOUTH!

Don't listen to him, he's full a shit. I won't let him lay a hand on you. . . . This fight is between you and me. . . .

Look, it's OK . . . it's OK . . . all youse gotta do is apologize to me and everything'll be cool, all right? Just get down on your knees and apologize and—

RICHIE! STAY OUT OF IT! . . . PUT IT BACK. . . . Put the blade back in ya pocket. . . .

Now Mike, look what you started, everybody's gettin' excited around here. Richie's gettin' angry, next thing Joey's gonna get angry. . . . Just get down on ya knees and apologize and then Richie won't think I'm an asshole. . . .

(condescendingly) That's great. . . . Just for a second . . . just stay down there for a second. . . . YA NOT A HOMO, ARE YA MIKE? Hey Joey, this guy down on his knees ya think maybe he's a homo? Haha. . . . And do me a favor while you're down there. Just slip your shoes off for a minute, will ya? Joey! Get the shoes! . . . You comfortable there, Mike? You're sure ya not a faggot, are you? You better not be, walking around this neighborhood. We'll castrate ya!

Here Mike, get up. You don't want to stay down there all day. Let me brush you off. Hey Mike, we're just fucking with ya head. You can take a joke, can't you? Sure you can! I wanna tell you something, Mike: you're good shit. Anytime you need anything in this neighborhood, you just come see me, Sonny, and I'll take care of you, OK? You need fireworks, anything like that, you come see me, OK? OK! (*shaking hands with him*) Well, it was nice talking to you, but we gotta get going, I'll see ya later. . . .

Hmmmm? What? What shoes? (*turning back to Joey*) These shoes? These are my shoes, Mike. These are my C-shoes. I just bought these shoes up in Bloomingdale's. Joey? Richie?

(*looks down at Mike's feet*) Oh, you don't got no shoes! Hey Joey, lookit dis guy's got no shoes! Richie, look! . . . Hey, how come you got no shoes? . . . All those nice clothes and no shoes! How'd dat happen? You're gonna get cold with no shoes! Ain't he gonna get cold?

(*laughing right into Mike's face*) Oh! I think we got a crybaby here! I think he's gonna start crying. (*Suddenly Sonny stops laughing, gets a very cold look in his eyes.*) Hey Richie, did you hear that? What was that word he just said?

(*lunging for Mike, grabbing him and talking slowly*) Hey Mike, we don't like swearing around here. Huh? Fuckface? Scumbag? (*fast, dangerous, pulling him up off the ground, so that we can see Sonny's eyes just over his fists*) Hey, hey. You come walking around this neighborhood, embarrassing me around my friends, swearing at me in front of my friends, hey let me tell you something, Mr. Nice Shoes, Mr. Faggot: You worried about not having no shoes? You're lucky you still got feet! (*Pause; he throws Mike to the ground.*) Get the fuck out of here! (*pause*) Asshole! . . . Come on. (*laughing as he walks away with Richie and Joey*) . . . Joey, lemme see my shoes. . . .

PARTY!

A man bops around the stage, preening.

Yo! I'm standin' on a street corner, I'm lookin' good, I'm feelin' good. I'm thinkin' about sidewalks and saxophones! I'm thinkin' it's a beautiful summer's night. I got on my brand-new clothes. I got me a bottle of wine. I want to go out tonight! I wanna go out and par-tee! I got on my bran'-new shoes *(indicates shoes)*, got on my bran'-new pants *(indicates pants)*, got on my bran'-new shirt *(models shirt to audience)*. Check that shirt out.... Qiana, baby.... Same as silk, same as silk! Got on my bran'-new "doo," aftershave. *(does a jump and claps his hands)* Um! I'm too good to waste! I wanna go out tonight and party! I want to go dancin'! I wanna go rollerskatin'! I say, Lord above, I am all dressed up tonight, Lord, I am looking good, and I am feeling good. Look at me! Look at me! You can't even believe how good I look!

Lord, I need me a little girl. Where's my little girl, Lord? Where's my little girl? Where's my . . . *(He sees the girl of his dreams down the sidewalk.)* . . . There she is jus' a-walkin' down the street! There she is jus' a-struttin' down the street! She got on them high-heeled shoes, swishy skirt, see-through blouse, lipstick, perfume . . . *(inhales the scent of the girl as she passes him along the apron of the stage)* . . . Hey, baby, hold on jus' a minute, where you goin' to? What's your name? You're looking good, and I'm looking good, whatchoo say we go get some Chinese food, go bowling?

Hey, baby, don't pass me by, I'm the superfly, I'll make you fly. . . . Yo! Sister! I wanna ask you a question: You know what time it is? (*He is now shouting at her retreating figure.*) Yo, sister! Yo, sister! Yo, BITCH, get yo ass back here, I'm talkin' to you! Hey! Come on, baby, whaddya say, we'll have a good time? (*pause*) Yeah, I know your type, twenty bucks, right? (*He turns away.*) Who the hell she think she is? (*turns back shouting*) Who the hell you think you are? Miss America or something? You got no right walkin' around looking like that! Enticing men. . . . Slut! Whore! Prostitute! . . . Ruined my whole evening!

FANTASY

A man sits, bent over, breathing hard.

Slut...bitch...cunt....Good magazine, yeah....Gina, huh? Virgin, huh? Yeah, I bet you make it with the whole football team. Ya slut. Yeah, spread 'em baby, come on full-color, yeah, let's see 'em....Yeah....Good magazine, yeah....

Yeah....I do it to you, ya slut, I know what you want, huh? I know what kind of guy ya like....I'm gonna make you scream 'cause I'm that kind of guy.

This ya girlfriend, huh? Huh? She's a real blonde, I can see that...couple of lesbos, that's what ya are! Whatchoo gonna do with that flashlight, huh? Yeah, I like ya both....

Especially you, Gina, ummmmm, you're nice, Gina....I like you, Gina....I like you, Gina, you're nice....I like you, Gina....I like you, Gina....I like you, Gina.... (coming) Uhhhhh....I like you, Gina....Uhhhhhhh....Ohhhhh! I LOVE YOU, GINA.

HELD DOWN

A man turns quickly, while seated.

Forget it! Just forget it, OK? No, I don't want a neck rub, Cheryl. No, I don't want a back rub either. No, I don't want that rubbed either, I don't want anything rubbed right now, keep your rubbing to yourself. Leave me alone. Don't touch me. . . . I know I know I know. . . . I'm sorry, OK? Is that what you want me to say? I'm sorry. . . .

(*pause*) Listen, Cheryl, we've got to get something straight between us, OK?. . . Every night can't be like last Wednesday night, all right? I have a lot of things on my mind, I've been working hard lately, I'm tired and that party tonight didn't help things. . . . I know, I know, I know it's not important, I know you don't care. . . . I don't care, nobody cares, all right?

It's just sex. What do we need sex for? We're just having a sexual relationship. What do we need sex for? Let's just play Trivial Pursuit for an hour or so. . . . I know I'm being childish. . . . I know. . . . You're right, it happens to every guy once in a while. Every guy once in a while can't. . . . It's normal, it's natural. . . . It happens to every guy. . . . Every guy once in a while, it's normal, it's natural, it happens to every guy. . . . SHIT! It doesn't happen to every guy, it happens to me. It happens to me. It's ME, it's ME, it's ME, it's me . . . and it's you, Cheryl. . . . No, no lemme talk. . . .

At the party tonight you spent the whole night hanging out with Robert in the kitchen. I saw you. Giving him those eyes, those "guess what I'm thinking about" eyes. All right, you're attracted to Robert. I understand. He just got that promotion, he's got a lot of money now, a lot of prestige, power, cocaine. What else could a girl want? Money, power, prestige, cocaine. I know what turns you on, Cheryl, I know because it's what turned you on about me in the first place. And I'm glad Robert got that promotion. Good. It couldn't have happened to . . . I'm glad he got that promotion. Fine. Good. Yes, Robert got that promotion. He got it because he's a back-stabbing, ass-licking slime. . . .

OK? OK? I could have gotten that promotion. I could have gotten it. But see, I have a little problem. I have too much integrity, see? I've got too many principles. My problem is that I go into work every day and I sit at my desk and like a sucker I try to do the best job I can. I sit at my desk eight hours a day, knock myself out and everybody sits at their desks and they watch me work. Because they know they're not as good as I am so they're afraid of me, so they watch me. They conspire against me because they're inferior. I am surrounded by a conspiracy of mediocrity just trying to hold me down, hold me down, HOLD ME DOWN, HOLD ME DOWN. . . .

(looks at his lap, stops shouting)

You know what your problem is, Cheryl? You're insatiable. You're never satisfied. You can't get enough. No guy is good enough for you. He has to be a success in the daytime, he has to be a success at night. He has to be a superman and a super-stud. You don't need a man, you need a machine. No wait, I know what you need, you need a real insensitive, male-chauvinist-pig cowboy. That's what you need. With the spurs. . . . Yeah, a real cowboy. . . .

RODEO

Very fast-paced, jittery, jumping around the stage. Highpitched "cowboy voice."

Whooooeeeee! Boy you shoulda been there, we took that sucker down! It was good, it was real good! (*moves his hands as if he's steering a car*) RRRRRMMMMM!!! Ninety-five miles an hour—BOOM! I hit that Winnebago, guy never knew what hit 'er! Just pushed 'im right off the side of the road.

I'm lookin' in my rearview mirror and I see that guy—he's jumped out of his car, jumpin' up and down, pissed off! I couldn't resist: I bang a U-ey, come back beside him and get out. Guy says to me, (*in deep Texas accent*) "Come here boy, I wanna talk to you!" I said, "I wanna talk to you too!" (*a right, a left*) BING! BANG! Guy never knew what hit him! Left enough rubber on that road to make a new set of tires!

I tell you, when it gets goin' that fast and hard I get high! Musta been doin' two, three hundred per. . . . Billy was pullin' 'em so fast he broke a knuckle. . . . You know that Billy when he starts pullin' those beers, pullin' those beers . . . jus' sittin' in the backseat like a hog in a corncrib, suckin' down that brew, half-naked, covered with sweat and stink. . . .

The beer cans rollin' aroun' on the floor and I musta been doing a hundred and fifty m.p.h.! . . . All of a sudden, I see this girl walkin' down the street, right? I couldn't resist. . . . I hit the brakes and start followin' her in the car, real slow like. Real Playboy-bunny type of girl, you know? I'm followin' real slow, givin' her my "evil eye" and she's jus' a-walkin' down the side-walk like she don't notice!...

All of a sudden, Billy pops out the back window: "Hey baby, hey baby, come 'ere, I wanna kiss your face!" She says, "Kiss my ass!" So Billy, you know what Billy says??? You know what he says? "I can't tell the difference!" I can't tell the difference! Pretty good, huh? That Billy's some kind of comedian, huh? Some kind of comedian. "I can't tell the difference!" WHOOOOEEEE!

(With no warning, he violently starts miming shooting a rifle three times in three different directions.) BOOM! BOOM! BOOM! Wished I had a machine gun, coulda killed me even more deer.... Killed me three deer, had to leave two behind! Didn't have room on the car for 'em! I jus' took this one big bloody buck, took him and strapped him onto the front of the car, tied him right onto the bumpers. So I'm goin' down the highway, musta been doin' three, four hundred miles per hour.... Billy's passed out in the backseat, and the blood starts comin' right up onto the windshield! I had to use my windshield wipers jus' so I could see! *(laughing)*

I come into this gas station—car's all covered with blood, right?—come into this gas station and the boy says to me: "You boys look like you been busy!" Billy hangs his head out the window like some kind of old dog, he says: "Sure have!" and pukes all over the guy's shoes! Whoooooeeeee!!! We know how to have a good time!

CHRISTMAS TREE

Middle-aged man, slumped in a chair.

Vinnie, Vinnie, Vinnie, Vinnie.... When you gonna get married, huh? When you gonna settle down.... You come in here every Monday morning with that bum friend of yours ... what's-his-name the alcoholic there, what's-his ... Tommy ... Tommy the alcoholic! You come in here every Monday morning, you been screwing this chick, you been screwing that chick ... you been drinking, you been wasting ya paycheck....

Hey, hey, Vinnie, ya twenty-eight years old, you're a bum.... You understand me? Uh? You're a bum and that friend a yours Tommy, he's a bum too ... and my kid Tony, he's a bum too. You're all bums. Bunch a bums. No sense a responsibility, nothin'. My kid Tony, seventeen and a half years old. He's got whatever he wants to have. Upstairs his own bedroom, his own cable TV, Space Invasion ... seventeen and a half years old he's playing with toys....

For his birthday he wants, he wants a 'lectric guitar, so we buy him a 'lectric guitar.... He's down in the basement till two o'clock in the morning playing the goddamn thing. Driving everybody crazy. Dog's barkin', everybody's awake.

You see my LTD out here? Who put the dent in my LTD? Who put the dent in that? Mister Punk Rock. "You got insurance, Dad," he says to me, "you got insurance"! ... I come home the other day from work, four-thirty in the afternoon ... he's lying on the couch like some kind of old man. I says to him, "Tony, what are you doin' lying on the couch? Go do your chores!" He says to me, "I did my chores, Dad." I says, "What chores, what chores you do around this house? Tell me, I want to know. . . ."

He says to me, "I fed the dog, Dad." I fed the dog!? I give a shit that dog starves to death! He fed the dog! What is that? He's got no responsibility!

When I was his age, Vinnie, when I was his age every day after school I had to go down to da Big Bear market and load boxes fa a buck an hour, a buck an hour. That was my responsibility. . . . My mother was sick, my brothers was no good. Every day.

And when I got outa high school I got drafted and I went to Korea. You know what Korea was? A war, smart-ass. . . .

I went to Korea and I served my country. That was my responsibility. . . .

And when I come back, everybody I knew was getting married . . . eh! I got married too. . . . I didn't know what the hell I was doin' . . . but I'll tell you something, Vinnie, it was the best thing I ever did in my life. The best thing. And you wanna know why? I'll tell you why. . . .

'Cause a Christmas. 'Cause a Christmas morning. . . .

Christmas morning, ya get up nice and early in the morning, ya know, with ya wife? And ya come downstairs and ya put the presents under the tree, ya know? And ya got the tree all lit up with the little bulbs and the tinsels and the lights dere? I like dose Christmas trees, gifts underneath all nice and shiny. And you have a nice cup a coffee and you have ya bathrobe on, and ya just sittin' dere nice and quiet on da couch with the wife . . . the oil burner's on. . . . And dose kids come runnin' down da stairs all happy and laughin' and da dog's barkin' and everybody's tearin' up dere presents and everybody's happy. And dose kids look up at you and dey love you. Dey love you, Vinnie. . . .

And den and den dere's Christmas dinner and everybody comes over da house. Ya mother and ya brothers and ya sisters and the kids and everybody's sitting around eatin' whatever they want to eat. . . .

And I sit there at that table, Vinnie, and I look at my family and I think to myself: All this belongs to me. This is my house, this is my family, this is my food on the table, goddamned dog on the floor. . . . It's all mine, it all belongs to me, Vinnie. . . .

And it makes me feel good inside, you know. It makes me warm.

That's why you gotta get married, Vinnie, you don't get married you're never gonna have a Christmas tree. Single guys, they don't got Christmas trees. . . .

LOOKING OUT FOR NUMBER ONE

A man on a stage talks to a small audience.

I want you all to do something for me right now. . . . I want you to take a look at the person sittin' next to you. Go ahead, don't be shy. . . . And now I want you to answer a question for me: What do you see? Do you see a success story? Do you see a potential millionaire? And what does your neighbor see when he looks at you? What do you see when you look in the mirror in the morning? Do you see a success? S-U-C-C-E-S-S! Success, that is what we are here to talk about tonight. . . .

There is only one person in this world who really matters: yourself! It is your job, it is your daily task to do one very simple and obvious thing: look out for number one. The world follows certain rules, certain laws. . . . And the first law has been the same since Adam and Eve: survival of the fittest! If you want the best for you and yours, you will remember that one fact. . . .

Now, I go to work every day. I'm given a job and I do it, I do it the best I can. . . . I go all over this great country of ours and I talk to people just like you: good, solid, white, middle-class Americans. I talk to them about success. That's my job. At the end of the week, I'm given a paycheck. That money belongs to me. I earned it, I deserve it! I don't ask for charity, I don't ask for a handout! I don't go down to some government office and ask them to pay my bills for me, no sir!! I am a member in good standing of the free-enterprise system. (*pause*)

I used to be ashamed that I owned a big home with a swimming pool. I used to be ashamed that I owned two beautiful cars: a Mercedes, and the Eldorado I saw many of you admiring as you came into the building. . . . I used to be ashamed that my children went to a school free of disagreeable influences . . . that we lived in a neighborhood free of disagreeable influences. . . . I felt guilty that we ate roast beef on Sunday afternoons! . . . Well, let me tell you something, friends. . . . We do not live in the Garden of Eden. We live right here on earth! And some will suffer, while others prosper, as it is written in the Bible.

Now, if you could ask the most successful men who ever lived, "What is the secret? What is the secret of success?" Ask Andrew Carnegie . . . ask John D. Rockefeller . . . ask Bob Hope. . . . If you could ask them, what would they tell you? They would tell you that there are two kinds of people in this world: there are the haves and the have-nots. Do you want to be a have? Do you want to look at this world from the bottom lookin' up or from the top lookin' down? 'Cause if you do, if you do you better get out there and you better get a piece of what belongs to you. . . . You want the good things in this world you better get out there, you better hustle! 'Cause if you don't, if you don't, you will be a have-not; and if you are a have-not, you can only lose. . . . If you are hungry, no one will feed you. . . . If you are hurt, no one will take care of you. . . . If a great storm comes from above and destroys the very home you live in . . . no one will replace it, no one will care. Unless you care. Unless you've taken care to take care of number one!

All kinds of people in this world: there are the poor, the foolish, the stupid, the crippled, the elderly. . . . Nothing you can do about them. . . . They've always been around, they're always gonna be around. The bleeding-heart liberals think you should take care of those who can't take care of themselves . . . the haves think you are responsible for the have-nots! You are responsible for only one person: yourself.

You are brought into this world as a single individual, you will live your life as a single individual. You will enjoy your own joy and you will experience your own pain. . . . Life is a struggle, man is an island. . . . Love . . . love, my friends, love is loving yourself first. Thank you, Amen.

VOICES OF
AMERICA

Voices of America premiered at Van Lagestein's Corps de Garde in Groningen, Holland, in April 1982.

WXXX

Fast, smooth, modulated.

Hey, we've got fifteen lucky winners every hour on the hour here at WXXX ROCK RADIO! (*singers: "W-X-X-X!"; sound effect*) Karen Sousa just won twenty-five dollars and free tickets to see the STONES at the Meadowlands this weekend. Say "Hi!" to Mick for me, Karen! Remember, there's winners every hour on the hour AND we'll be giving away the MADNESS (*horn*) TEN-THOUSAND-DOLLAR PRIZE sometime this week. Listen up, answer the question of the day and YOU may be a winner! I'm John Cummmmmmmmings and we'll be rockin' out all afternoon! (*singers: "W-X-X-X! MORE MUSIC!"*) We've got the request line open and . . . WHAT!? Oh, I'm supposed to ask the question NOW? OK, here's the question. . . . If you had a choice of dying from a NUCLEAR HOLOCAUST (oh, no!) or a HEROIN OVERDOSE (oh, wow!), which would you choose? Just joking! The question is: Dum-de-de-dumm-dumm-da! WHAT is KEITH RICHARD'S hairdresser's name? Know the answer? OK, OK . . . donnnnn't tell anybody! We're keeping the lines open and the first fifteen listeners to call in will WIN tickets to see the STONES and a chance at the MADNESS (*horn*) TEN-THOUSAND-DOLLAR PRIZE. . . . Buys a lot of balloons. (*buzzer*) Gotcha! Hey! It's two-thirty, school's out, it's a beautiful day, well I promised it to you, I said I'd have it and listen we're gonna HAVE that EXCLUSIVE . . . John . . . Lennon . . . interview. . . . Just minutes before he died. It's coming up in the next hour. . . . But first . . . a word from Ernie. . . .

NEW ACTION ARMY

A young male voice.

Hey! Can I ask you a question? Are you a confused young guy? Don't know where you're going? Can't find a job? Lonely?

How'd you like a job where you travel all over the world, learn a skill, wear a uniform, meet a bunch of great guys and even earn a little money?

If your answer is "Yes!" you might be the kind of guy we're looking for for the NEW ACTION ARMY. . . .

How'd you like to handle a real weapon? See the world? PLUS you get a uniform that's recognized just about everywhere . . . and you meet a bunch of great guys who like to have fun and drink.

The best part is, it's exciting . . . you're risking your life twenty-four hours a day.

So whaddya say? The army's a lotta fun! Come on and be a part of it!

The New Action Army—Where the Action Is!

(deep male voice tag)

Call your local recruiter for details today.

SALE, SALE, SALE!

Very, very fast, loud, nonstop.

Sale, sale, sale, sale, sale, sale! Come on down girls, we've got great savings, great buys 'cause it's SUMMERTIME DOLLAR-DAYS DISCOUNTS this month at ZEEBO'S Department Stores!

Ready for summer barbecues? We are, with nifty hibachis, fully automatic gas-driven barbies, electric charcoal cookers and portable turning spits. All on sale with colorful matching accessories: racks, forks, aprons, lawn chairs. Start your garden now. We've got seeds, hoses, shovels . . . all you add is the elbow grease. . . . But make sure you're dressed right: we've got sunhats, sea socks and sand shoes on sale now! Watch the figure, girls: sexy squeeze girdles, and extra-sharp pointed Dardee uplift padded underwire support bras, disposable nylon stockings, on sale now! And for Junior, matching play clothes, pail-and-shovel set, harness and tether! Don't forget Dad: We've got tools for the car, adjustable liquor cabinets and, just in this week, bowling shoes and fabulous fishing hats! Gramma wants to come along? She'll need a cane, maybe a wheelchair . . . all on sale! We've got realistic leatherette bones for Fido, electric guitars for the young rockers, and fully automatic submachine guns for Uncle!

Sale, sale, sale, sale, sale, sale! We've got barbecues galore and all the trimmings 'cause it's Summertime Dollar-Days Discounts this month at all Zeebo's Department Stores!

Better hurry!

LI'L DOGGIE DOG FOOD

Deep Texas drawl, Rawhide.

(sound effect of cattle)

HEYAAAH! HEYAAAH! Git on there, li'l dogies!

(dog bark) Hi there, fella! *(bark)*

(chuckle) Being a working cowboy is no easy job. . . . I'm roping cattle from sunup to sundown, keeping those lil' dogies in line. . . . That's why I got my partner here, King. *(bark)* . . . Heh heh. . . . He works hard too!

At the end of the day, when I'm ready to eat a nice big steak, well you know, King is pretty hungry too. . . . *(bark)* Heh heh. . . . That's why I give him Li'l Doggie Dog Food—all meat, chunks of beef! Hell, he's around those cows all day long . . . you bet he wants to eat one! *(bark)*

That's why he gets the real thing, the best thing: pure, one hundred percent, grade-A, all-American prime beef! Those Hindus won't touch it, but hell, my dog sure will!

(bark) My dog's a working man . . . he deserves to eat like a man. Doesn't your dog deserve the same? Li'l Doggie all-beef dog food—for the little man in the house. . . . *(bark)* Heh heh . . . HEYAAAH!!! *(cattle sound)*

REAL ITALIAN

This is Mario at Mario's Real Italian Restaurant.

We got clams! We got lobsters! We got spaghetti, anchovies, lasagna, soup de jour! We got the best cooks in town, the best sauce, the best garlic bread.

And don't forget Mario's "Mama Mia" salad bar with all the radishes, carrots, shrimps, Bac-o-Bits, lettuce, cottage cheese, swiss squares, celery sticks, swedish meatballs, cucumbers, croutons, and ten different dressings you can eat!

You wanna eat? You wanna eat till you DIE? Come on down to Mario's Real Italian—Route 115 and the Old Colony Turnpike behind Bamberger's in Paramus!

We'll feed you like your mama used to! *Mangia!*

(*new voice*) Open for lunch and dinner. All major credit cards accepted!

WFRO

Smooth Latin accent.

Let me ask you something: Are you in a dead-end job? Don't you wish you were a rich guy? Don't you wish you had the good things in life? A nice car. A big stereo. A hot chick? Hey, if you were a radio announcer you'd have them. Because radio announcers have a great time—look at me: Roco; I'm the proof, baby!

OK, you want to become a hot DJ—you better get on the phone and call the NBC school for radio broadcasting. They have a special three-week course, tells you everything you need to know, you know? And then, they help you get a job! Hey, and if you're a veteran, you may be eligible for their special handicapped veteran program. So stop wasting your time, call the NBC Radio Announcers School right now at 212-555-7757. . . . Hey, and tell 'em Roco told you about it, OK?

OK! You're listening to Roco, the voice of disco on WFRO. I hope you are all out there hot and ready for some hot disco dancing because we got the hits for you tonight! . . . I know the girls are HOT, because I feel HOT and when I feel HOT everything I touch gets HOT and I'm touching some hot new record, just came in today, you be hearing it this weekend at the DISCO. . . . This is the Hell's Kitchen Gang . . . bringing it home to you, mama. It's called "Watch the Red!"

WATCH THE RED!

Done as a rap, with a beat.

I said "Watch the Red! Watch the Red! Watch the Red! Watch
the Red!"
Best keep watchin' till you lose bread,
Said I rock you here, I rock you dere,
I rock you right outa your underwear!
I said some are hot, and some are cold, but
I keep a-rockin' till I'm rock-and-rolled
Said Uptown, Downtown, 'Roundtown Saturday Night,
If you don't know which way is up, baby you ain't too bright!
This is a story without much glory, it happened just the other
night,
I was in the big city, feelin' real pretty, stopped at a traffic
light....
A chick walked by, I said my, my...that lady is outasight
The girl's chunky but funky, she's movin' I'm groovin'
I wanna go PARTY tonight!
So I says to the dame, What's your name, Lady Jane?
I'm the superfly, I can make you fly
How 'bout a movie, or somethin' groovy?
Chinese food? Or a Quaalude....Are you in the mood? Are
you in the mood?
I gunned my engine, I wanted attention and I wanted it right
away!
But she kept walkin', she heard me talkin', but man, that chick
was gay!
Life in the city, it sure ain't pretty
It gets me down, this crazy town

It's makes me feel so blue, like I'm in a zoo
Like I'm in a cage, like I'm in a rage
I wanna pull the plug, take a slug
End it all, 'cause I feel real small
I feel all alone, I got no home,
I might as well be livin' in the twilight zone!

FAT FIGHTER

Fat-fat-fat-fat-fat-fat-fat....

Take a look in the mirror, what do you see? A slim, shapely, sensuous woman? A woman who attracts men when she walks down the street?

Or do you see fat?

Around the neck, around the thighs, around the waist.... What about your wrists, your ankles, your cheeks? Look carefully, fat is everywhere....

If you're fat, you need help. You need...FAT FIGHTER, the new proven formula that dissolves fat as it accumulates. Now you can eat as much as you like all day long and not gain a pound. Just take two FAT FIGHTERS before you start eating, then eat ice cream, cake, candy, butter, potato chips, spaghetti, beer, thick cream soups, pies, heavy breads, french fries, syrups, puddings, lard, milkshakes, fudge, chocolates, pancakes, waffles, pâté, oil, grease, pizza, cookies...and not gain a pound!

Fat Fighter is all you need...and it's guaranteed....

And remember, FAT FIGHTER contains no harmful ingredients, just pure one-hundred-percent dextroamphetamine sulfate.

FAT FIGHTER...when you're FAT FAT FAT!

THE CRASH

(*Station ID voice: "More music-XXX!"*) Yeah . . . hey, we still got a couple a minutes on the MADNESS phone and while we're waiting for your call . . . hey, you know one of my favorite political rock groups today is The Crash. Yeah . . . really make me think about things, you know what I mean? I listen to their lyrics and I get mad . . . they're real. And we've got a real surprise for you, a real recording of The Crash when they were playing that great benefit concert for all the starving people in . . . uh . . . wow, I forgot where! Anyway, it was great, they're great, and this is one of their great songs: "We're Not Gonna Take It Anymore. . . ."

(*Live concert-audience effect: cheering, whistles, etc. Man with Cockney accent addresses the audience.*)

Thank you. Thank you. (*spits*) Thank you. This next tune is dedicated to all the people fighting in El Salvador, Northern Ireland and the South Bronx. It's called "We're Not Gonna Take It Anymore!"

(*screaming*)

I said a one, two, three, four—we're not gonna take it anymore!
Five, six, seven, eight—(*knocks*) We're knocking, knocking at your door. . . .

(*chorus*) Who's there? Who's there? Who's there?
Better let us in, or we'll blow it in!

With guns in hand we'll roam the land. . . .
We'll find the cheats with their Parliament seats. . . .
We'll knock 'em down and we'll hang 'em high. . . .
And they'll say "My, my!" as they slowly die. . . .
I said a one, two, three, four!

Thank you . . . thank you . . . thank you. . . .

TWENTY-FIVE TOP DEAD

Twenty-five top dead recording artists—rock, pop, jazz, folk, new wave: all DEAD, all GOLD, all IMMORTAL!

(*music collage over*)

Buddy Holly!

This is a limited-time offer, a special two-album set of the greatest hits by the greatest martyrs of music. All dead! All gold! All immortal!

Just listen to what you get! John Lennon!

But that's not all! You also get Janis Joplin, Jimi Hendrix, jazz great John Coltrane. Yes, you get Phil Ochs, Mama Cass, Elvis Presley . . . and who can forget Mario Lanza. . . .

Also Sid Vicious, Darby Crash, Tim Buckley, Duane Allman and Berry Oakley. Grateful Dead's Pigpen, Otis Redding, James Honeyman-Scott, Mark Bolan and the entire T-Rex. . . . Yes you get Bob Marley, Harry Chapin, Eric Dolphy. . . . Twenty-five top dead recording artists, all GOLD, all DEAD! Yes, you get Jim Morrison, AC/DC's immortal Bon Scot, Keith Moon, Brian Jones, Richard Farina, Nat King Cole and who can forget Eddie Cochrane?

Led Zeppelin's legendary Jon Bonham. . . .

This special memorial album is not available in record stores, only through this special TV offer for only $19.95!

Call toll-free, 1-800-555-7757, or send check or money order to:

MUSIC MARTYRS! PO Box 25, John F. Kennedy Station, NY, NY 10099.

Act now and receive your special bonus comedy album: John Belushi and Lenny Bruce "Live!" This is a limited-time offer, it may not be around tomorrow, call today!

UNCOLLECTED

Occasionally I will work on a monologue, only to find that it doesn't fit the longer solo performance. It becomes an orphan.

I have collected some of these monologues here. They are raw. They have not had the benefit of repeat performances.

"Confession," "Dope" and "Just Business" were destined to be part of *Drinking in America* and never made it. "A Great Bunch of Guys" was originally performed as a voice-over to a slide show in *Men in Dark Times* (1982). "The Stud" was part of the touring solo entitled *That Girl* (1980). "The Throat" and "Alone Together" showed up in *Advocate*, an X-rated collection of pieces at Artist's Space (1983). And "The Quiet Man" was removed from *FunHouse* in its first run at the Public Theater.

CONFESSION

In the name of the Father, the Son and the Holy Ghost, Amen. Dear Lord . . . forgive me for I have sinned. I have done many bad things this past week. Things that I am almost afraid to confess. . . . O Lord Jesus, have mercy on my poor soul. Please show me the love that you have shown for the vilest leper and the most wretched whore. . . .

Jesus, I have sinned. I have been drunk twice this week. And while I was drunk, I smoked a lot of cigarettes and I swore. I told a story that mocked black people and that made fun of a woman's breasts. . . .

Jesus, I have sinned. After I was drunk, I drove home and I broke the speed limit and tried to run over a dog. And I took your name in vain. Jesus, forgive me.

And Jesus, I have been gluttonous too. On Thursday night while I was watching TV I ate an entire carton of ice cream, two bags of potato chips and eleven Slim Jims.

Also I have been lecherous, Lord. The same night I watched the Mandrell sisters on television and imagined them naked and making lesbian love to one another. . . .

And Jesus, a man in my office was promoted over me, and I wished that I had the promotion instead. And I cursed him.

But Lord, my worst sin is hard for me to say. . . . I had a fantasy, Lord. I had a fantasy about that guy in the office. I had a fantasy that he and I were alone together after work. And when he turned his back to me, I grabbed a pencil from my desk and stabbed him in the neck. And when he fainted, Lord, I tied his feet and hands to the desk. Then I poured lighter fluid over him, Lord . . . and . . . and while he was burning I popped his eyes out with a letter opener. Then I broke the blade off the paper cutter and sawed off his arms and his legs while he screamed. Then I ground the pieces up in a paper shredder and flushed them down the toilet. Then I took his still screaming torso and compacted it in a trash compactor. . . .

O Lord, forgive me, I have sinned. . . .

DOPE

Mellow, hip voice.

Okay man, come on up....Don't worry. Don't worry! The dog's in the bedroom....I promise she won't bite you, I just fed her. Just come on up....You don't have anyone with you? Good.

So what do you need? I got Thai stick, Hawaiian, Jamaican and Napa Valley....The Hawaiian is very green, gives a very clean, fast head. And it's strong. The Jamaican is more mellow, more colors. I wouldn't buy this domestic unless you're having a big party or something and you just need a lot of industrial-grade smoke around....The Thai is good. Thai is always good. Guy who gets it for me actually goes to Bangkok to pick it up.... Really....He's very cool, been doing it for years....Keeps all his money in precious jewels. Says he'll take me someday....I know what you like....If I were you I'd go with the Hawaiian. You can't go wrong with Hawaiian. You won't fall asleep, but it's very strong. One hit. Yeah. Here, I'll roll one, you can try it....And you want a quarter, right? Cool.

What else can I do you for? Heh heh....

No problem. Yeah, a gram doesn't last too long these days.... I've got two things, actually the same thing, but not really: I've got pink Peruvian flake, excellent. Here take a look, excellent, you can see the color...lovely stuff....That's powder, probably has some cut in it, I never cut it, but that's the way it comes and you never know. . . . That's a C-note a gram for that. Simple, straightforward blow. . . .

Then I've got the rocks. These are real rocks, very clean, very pure. . . . A guy I know shoots and he only does this stuff. . . no adulterants whatsoever. Two hundred a gram. . . . Well, this is close to pure, that's why. This is the blow that a certain first-baseman used to do. . . follow my drift? Smoking coke. . . yeah. Go for it. You only live once. Here, let me weigh it up. You'll see it comes to a lot.

What else do you need? 'Ludes? I got pharmaceutical 'ludes. . . . Ecstasy? . . . Have you tried it yet? I'm waiting until this weekend, go to Palladium and flip out. Should be nice. . . . Valiums I got. Tuinals, got trouble sleeping? . . .

Hey, wait a minute, I got something you have to try . . . this is very special . . . have you ever tried heroin? . . . No, I know, I feel the same way, but this is different stuff, this is pure.

The heroin you read about is that street shit. . . . Half the time it isn't even heroin, it's quinine mixed with barbiturates or powdered methadone or one of those things.

I'm talking about USDA-approved, grade-A, pure heroin. This stuff just doesn't exist anymore. And I know what you're thinking, because I was thinking the same thing: No needles for me, thank you. But see, that's what junkies use 'cause they do that garbage street stuff. This is pure, this is like what a doctor would give you in the hospital. It's completely different. Much more like opium, and you know opium's cool. And you don't shoot it, see? No, you don't snort it either. . . . You smoke it on a piece of tinfoil. Very clean and sanitary. It's good for you, lets you get into your head. . . .

Here, just try a little bit, it won't kill you. It's very nice, it's like smoking very mellow weed. Check it out. . . .

JUST BUSINESS

Man on the phone. Hearty, big voice.

Yeah, OK, put him on...yeah....JACK! How ya doin'? Yeah...yeah....Doin' real great....Yeah, she's good, so's the kids...yeah....

What's on your mind...what can I do for you?...Yeah.... Yeah, I know....Yeah, it's kind of sticky....Yeah *(stretching as he talks)*...Yeah, I can see what you're saying....Well, but, yeah, Jack....Jack, I think it's great that you're sticking up for the guy, I mean I really appreciate it, I really...

It's good to hear your point of view, Jack, you know I respect your opinion on things....Yeah....Yeah...but listen, Jack....Jack, I like Barry too, OK, but I had to let him go because, look, he's just not...yeah, but he's not producing, Jack! He's not profitable....

Jack, the guy's fifty-nine years old and he doesn't come in and do a day's work! We all gotta pull our weight around here.... Jack, the amount of money I'm paying him, I can hire three kids out of college who will hustle and break their little behinds right in two! Start 'em at 22K and watch 'em run!

Bushy tails and bright eyes are what I need, Jack, not the Geritol and shuffleboard set. What do I need the guy for? Yeah, I like the guy too. I've known him for twenty-three years. Our kids played ball together....

Yeah, but he, uh, Jack, LISTEN. . . . NO, he doesn't give me any alternative! I didn't want to fire him. I offered him a job in shipping, but he turned me down! He said he couldn't take the pay cut! Well, now he's got a pretty big pay cut if you ask me!

I know, I know . . . it's tough, but what else can I do? I can't pay a guy sixty-five thou a year to sharpen pencils and goose his secretary! I know he's got a pension coming up. . . . Well, Jack. . . . WHAT DO YOU WANT ME TO DO, FOR CRYING OUT LOUD? I'M NOT IN THE FUCKING WELFARE BUSINESS! I'M IN A PROFIT BUSINESS HERE!

Yeah, yeah. . . . Look, can I talk for two seconds, OK, please? Can I get a word in edgewise? All right, well just, follow me for a second, OK, just follow this logic, will ya? . . .

You like, you like that place you just bought up in the mountains? You like your swimming pool? You like that Mercedes station wagon your wife drives? You like having your kid in Exeter? Jack, listen, that stuff costs money and there's only one thing that makes money for you and that's this business.

Now, if you want to tell me that you want to trade your job for his job . . . because . . . BECAUSE THAT'S EXACTLY . . . THAT'S EXACTLY WHAT . . . THAT'S EXACTLY WHAT YOU'RE DOIN', JACK!

Jack, if we're not making money in this place I can't pay anybody, can I? Now, if you want to take a pay cut so I can keep Barry, be my guest . . . but that's the way the cookie crumbles and I'm sorry. I really am. You gotta look out for number one or there ain't gonna be no numbers at all, kid. . . .

Look, I got a call coming in in a few minutes so I better get off the phone. . . . I appreciate you sticking up for Barry, Jack, but in a funny way that makes me want to get rid of him even more, because now he's wasting your time as well! And I can't have people wasting time in this company . . . yeah . . . yeah. Well, lemme tell you, Jack, anytime you want a job in the personnel department. I can arrange it. . . . Just joking! Just joking! Yeah. Yeah. I know it gets a little out of hand sometimes, it gets a little crazy, I know. We've all been working hard. Yeah.

Yeah . . . I know. I know. . . . No, I don't blame you. OK. Yeah. So . . . so . . . say "Hi" to Jeanette for me, all right? Yeah. OK. OK. Yeah. Yeah. . . . OK . . . OK. . . . Yeah. . . . Bye. . . . Bye, Jack. OK. . . . Yeah, you too!

(hangs up)

A GREAT BUNCH OF GUYS

(from MEN IN DARK TIMES)

Every day, me and da fellas used ta get tagetha and go down to da docks. Dey were a bunch a hot shits, you know whud I mean?

Dere was Angie and Tony and Vinnie and Vito and me. Every day we'd go down ta see if dey had any woik for us. Some days dey did, and some days dey didn't. When dey did, we'd woik all day hauling coffee beans or tuna-fish heads or some shit like dat. For a buck an hour . . . a buck an hour.

But dat wasn't such bad money den. Nobody had any money and dey was honest. Not like dese crooks and bums you see around da streets dese days. Dey don't know da meaning a woik.

Some days we couldn't get no woik, so we'd hang around. Maybe, if Tony had some money—'cause he was kinda rich since his fadda had a grocery store—if Tony had some money, we'd go and buy donuts at da donut factory. We'd always make Vito ask for 'em, 'cause Vito stuttered and he had ta practice talkin', ya know. Except we all thought it was pretty funny.

Anyway, Vito died in da war. We all went over, but Vito was on da front and he got a bullet true da neck. Den we all came back afta da war and we didn't have nuddin' ta do. It was like a depression except nobody cared and we was all gettin' money for sittin' on our asses anyway.

Den Tony got married, den Angie got married. So I said, "Shit, what da hell!" and I got married too. Vinnie went ta college, da smart-ass. Den he got into da movies. Sometimes I see him on da late show. He always plays goombas, usually a criminal or sometin'.

So now, Angie's got cancer and once in a while I see Tony afta church when I get a paper at his store.

I don't know. It's funny. Dey were a bunch a great guys.

THE STUD
(from THAT GIRL)

A man addresses the audience in a slow, confident drawl.

Sometimes, when I'm in a bar, having a drink with some guys, one will make an idle comment like "How does he do it? He always has the girls. . . . "

I remain quiet when I hear such remarks. I tend to keep a low profile with regard to my "extracurricular activities." I don't need to advertise, I know what I've got . . . and the girls, they can tell by my eyes . . . they know what I've got. . . .

I'm not so good-looking. I was athletic when I was younger, but no Mr. Universe. I'm medium height and medium weight. I've never really excelled at anything, certainly not school, and as far as my job goes, they can all fuck themselves.

But you know what? I don't care. 'Cause I've got what every guy . . . and every woman wants . . . and all the looks, brains and money in the world can't buy it—I'm "endowed." I've got a long, thick, well-shaped prick. The kind girls die for. . . .

You're laughing. So what? Fuck you. Facts are facts. I'll hang out in a bar down on Wall Street around six or seven o'clock and in come the girls. The ones I like are the business types, the ones with their suits and big bow ties and Adidas. Shit. I'll wear a jacket and tie, nothin' fancy, I want 'em to know my politics. One way or the other I say a word or two to the chick and we end up either having another drink or splitting.

They love to tell me about their boyfriends and lovers. About what wonderful men they are. So nice, so gentle, so dependable...so boring. And they love to tell me what a wonderful cock I've got, so big, so hard, so unlike anything they've got at home. And to top it off, I've got a special surprise: I don't come for a long, long time...and when I do, there's more to follow....

Ever see a girl cry 'cause she's so happy? Ever see a girl beg to take another look? Ever see someone faint because she's had such an intense orgasm?...

I have....

Let's face it, sex is what everyone is basically interested in. Everybody wants great sex with great-looking great fucks. And there are only so many. And I am one.

It's like in college when I studied what's-his-name, the Greek guy, Plato. He said that everything in the world has a perfect example after which it is modeled. Platonic perfection, that's my sex life.

Don't tell me about love, I got love. I always keep the best for daily use, that's love....I got love...and I got all the others too....I see a girl walking down the street who appeals to me, next thing I know, I'm doing her...and she's loving it.

Some of 'em get scared after a while and go back to their boyfriends, that's fine with me. Some get addicted, I get rid of them too. One girl told me she was gonna kill herself....Never did find out what happened....

But most of the time they are very cool about it. Whenever I call 'em up, they drop whatever they're doing, whatever they're doing, and come to me. A couple of times girls have stopped fucking their boyfriends when I called. See, they understand that this kind of quality and quantity is in limited supply. . . .

I don't give out my phone number, I don't need the aggravation. No I don't need the aggravation . . . just the good part. . . .

THE THROAT

(from ADVOCATE)

Spoken formally.

I am constantly amazed, almost frightened, by the sensitive complexity of the human physical plant. The human body, that is.

Consider the throat. Normally used for transmitting air, food and speech, it is the body's most vital highway. It is nothing less than the path between heart and mind. And it must be kept in perfect working order, clean of debris, lubricated, warm and nourished.

It is esthetically pleasing as well. For the neck is one of the most graceful and erotic parts of the body. The slightest touch on the throat brings feelings of titillation and pleasure.

The throat is such a sensitive thing. A small disorder can cause a sore throat—or worse, a diseased throat. Fever and pain set in and, if they persist, the throat becomes a source of intense irritation.

It becomes the sole center of conscious attention. Imagine for a moment a canker in the throat. Sore and open. Deep inside. Burning. Or many cankers, inflamed and bleeding. The throat becomes dry as the pain increases. It is impossible to swallow.

Then the discovery that the cankers are malignant. Cancer of the throat. Life-threatening, it must be removed. Perhaps the vocal cords are destroyed in the process; a hole is left. A new voice is created. The whole personality changes. Crippled . . . perhaps no voice at all. Mute.

The throat is very vulnerable. It must be protected at all costs. Imagine being punched in the throat. Or strangulation. Asphyxiation. Tighter and tighter, then blackout.

A piece of wire is all that's needed. But perhaps the worst of all is the most spectacular: the slitting of the throat with a straight razor.

One deft move, deep and quick. The wound is fatal, yet consciousness persists. . . .

ALONE TOGETHER

(from ADVOCATE)

A man stands deep in the corner of the stage, almost mumbling, in a kind of "aw shucks" manner.

Hello, remember me? I'm right here where you left me. Right in that dark corner.... I've been waiting....

Come on, gimme a smile. You owe me that. After all this time. All my memories....

Wait, nothin' to be scared of. You know me...harmless. Nothin' but a joke. Always was, always will be....

You didn't think I was gonna stay way back there forever, did you? Huh. Pushing my broom. Hauling the big roller trash cart filled with used-up pint-sized milk cartons, scribbled paper, broken pencils, apple cores.... No, not forever.... Huh....

You may have forgotten me, but I remember. When you've got the time, you remember everything....

I even kept your picture. See?... Oh, you don't want to look? You don't like it? I do. I look at it all the time. Nice outfit...nice colors, school colors, right? I know....

It catches you just the way. That way you used to be. That smile. That laugh. I remember your laugh very well. Seems like you were always laughing.... You used to laugh at me kinda, huh?

Wait a minute, you just got here.... I wanna ask you.... You still that way? You're not laughin' now. You seem pretty serious now.... Why are you so serious?

We can have some fun....It's just you and me down here, you know....Funny you should come down here after all these years. But you know, I've always been here. Always....

Wait...I know...we can tell each other stories....

Well...about things that have happened. I bet a lot of interesting things have happened to you since then. You were always so interesting. You always had such interesting things to say....What? Sure, I heard you talking....And I remember every word. You and your friends had so much to say in those days, so young...so satirical....Huh?

I have a good memory. For stories.

Like one time, I was down here. All alone. Just about where you're standing right now, near that damp spot, and I heard this noise....Just a little noise. In the wall there....Scratchin'. Something scratchin' against metal....I almost stopped breathing.

Then I pulled that piece of metal back....Very slowly. As careful as I could. I looked in and it was dark, of course.

Up jumps this rat, right at my face....That was all it was. A rat. I killed it in one kick. Just a rat...huh.

It was so quiet down here and that rat went and bothered me with its scratchin'. Disturbed me, you know.

Like just now, it was real quiet and peaceful...and then, what do you know, there you were.

Just like it was yesterday....

THE QUIET MAN

(deleted from FUNHOUSE)

A man speaks to the audience in a very sincere, direct and quiet manner.

This is my place. Welcome to my place. This is the place where people come to watch people. People love to watch people, don't you think? I know I do. . . . There are so many, the variety is endless.

I can't imagine anything finer than a sunny Sunday afternoon in the park where I can just sit and watch the world go by. The young couples in love. The sturdy joggers. The pretty girls. And the children. I especially love to watch children playing. . . . The way they sort of tumble along, singing and laughing in little voices. . . . Everything is exciting and amusing, everything is new to them. Everyone's their friend.

"Little people." It's a miracle that hands could be so small and perfectly formed. Eyes so bright. Skin so fair. They haven't a care to wrinkle their small brows.

(pause)

Sometimes, one will come close by where I sit. Perhaps a little girl of nine years or so will come and quietly look at me. I can almost picture her now, the little rosebud of a mouth, the tummy thrust forward, the knobby knees peeking out from under a frilly dress. An angel come to visit.

How I memorize each feature as she stands before me; each gesture, each breath. If I sit very still, she might even speak to me. This is when I must be very gentle, careful not to scare her.

"Would you like to sit down?" I might ask.

She turns to see if Mother's watching, and then, like the little lady she is, she places her sweet bottom on the bench beside me. Then she asks me: "How old are you?" and I just smile. . . .

She reaches out and touches my hand, curious, yet so cautious. If I am really lucky, she doesn't let go.

We hold hands and watch the world go by together. . . . I look down at her shining hair, her barrette . . . the tiny, immaculate ear, the slender neck. So fragile. . . .

What could be better than this? To be so close to pure hope. . . .

(pause)

The mother calls. And my little friend, forewarned about the peril in our illicit love, runs off. . . .

As I wave good-bye.

A NOTE ON PERFORMANCE

Each piece takes place in a very spare set. Two chairs and a microphone and microphone stand for Drinking in America; a table, chair and table mic for FunHouse; one chair for Men Inside; a mic on a mic stand for Voices of America.

I always wear the same thing: black pants, a white oxford button-down shirt (sometimes a white T-shirt) and black ref shoes.

The idea is to perform athletically. Jump around. Scream and shout. Knock myself out. Go from one piece to the next rapidly and without pause.

I have a wide vocal range, which I make broader using a microphone. I usually "fake" some kind of accent: Texan, Southern, Black urban, Italo-ethnic . . . what feels right.

Many of the monologues address the audience directly, behind some conceit like lecturing or preaching. Occasionally I'm speaking to another person, but the amount of pantomime used to indicate that person is kept to a minimum.

I try to keep what I'm doing and what the character is doing in the same plane. I never make believe I'm doing anything, like driving a car. I'm not a mime. It's too distracting for the audience.

I try to get as close to the reality of the character as possible using only my voice, posture and inner feelings. Sometimes I feel the guy is standing next to me.